LET'S GROW!

Gardening in Dutchess County,

Written by the area's most
experienced farmers and gardeners

Edited by Mark Adams
Illustrated by Deanna Gotthardt

Published by Mark Adams Greenhouses, Inc.
© 1987
Printed in Poughkeepsie, N.Y.
By Hamilton Reproductions

DEDICATION

This book is dedicated to
my father, Ralph R. Adams
who taught me how to work.

Editor's Preface

This little book should be a companion to anyone who gardens, or is thinking of starting a garden, in Dutchess County. It doesn't answer every question about growing flowers, vegetables, trees and shrubs, and it doesn't explain in minute detail every nuance of soil preparation, mulching or pest control. What this book does offer is the advice and experience of the Hudson Valley's foremost farmers and gardeners, written in his or her own words, so that the reader can gain some insight into the world of gardening in one of the most beautiful of all garden spots--Dutchess County.

So, let's share the experience of gardening in Dutchess County, and, ---Let's Grow!

Acknowledgements

It took more than twelve gardeners to write this book. Most of the authors had lots of help from friends, fellow experts and an assortment of typists, proofreaders and advisors. The editor would like to thank all the authors, illustrators and their assistants, who were so enthusiastic about this project that the book practically wrote itself, and also graphic designer Cathy Wing, who was so helpful and patient while it all unfolded, literally, in front of her eyes. As editor, I also thank my wife Sue, who typed up the manuscripts, and my staff in the greenhouse, who did all the work while I was off playing publisher.

--Mark Adams

Contents

LIST OF ILLUSTRATIONS

1

A Glimpse into the Past

By Mark Adams

Let me tell you the tale of a part of my farm at Hyde Park for which I have a fairly clear record. It was settled about 1740; the trees were cut; the stumps removed, the fields planted. The Old Dutch and New England owners used rotation of crops--corn and wheat and rye and grass. They had cows, and manure from the barnyard was spread on the land. As late as 1840 that farm grew prize corn. But the toll had been taken and from then down to 1910, when I took hold of it, went from bad to worse...and now I am putting it into trees in the hope that my great-grandchildren will be able to try raising corn again--just one century from now.[1]

When President Franklin D. Roosevelt told this little "tale" in 1937, he was urging his audience, and all Americans, to join him in the crusade for natural conservation. And he was also offering a neat synopsis of the history of agriculture in his own Dutchess County.

HISTORY OF COMMERCIAL HORTICULTURE
EARLY SETTLERS

That history goes back to a time when Indians from the Wappingers and Algonkian tribes were dwelling on the banks of the Hudson River, fishing, hunting and farming on a small scale. The crops they raised probably included corn, beans, squash and pumpkins, and their only domesticated animal was the dog.

New England was already heavily populated with settlers of European descent when the first Dutch immigrants landed near present-day Fishkill. These early settlers, among them Francis Rombout and Gulian Verplanck, were fur-traders, exchanging goods with the Indians for highly-valued pelts which they shipped back to Europe. The Dutch did grow a few crops, including wheat, first planted in Dutchess County in 1626.[2]

PATENTS LOCK UP THE LAND

In order to keep the burgeoning population of Massachusettes and Connecticut from spilling over into New York, the colonial government granted huge tracts of land, or "patents" to the few families living along the eastern side of the Hudson. By 1703 eleven[3] patents had been granted in "Dutchess County", and fewer than 40 families were in permanent residence.

The powerful landlords of old Dutchess had little incentive to allow settlement of their property, since their primary interest was trading. The Livingston family did bring a group of persecuted German Palatines to settle near present-day Germantown, and they were engaged in making tar out of pine-pitch, paying rent to their landlords.[4] But many residents were squatters on the huge patents, and others moved onto tracts of land that had a disputed title. Naturally, little improvement was made to the land under these conditions, and agriculture remained primitive, limited mainly to subsistence farming.

RENT WAR

By 1765, anti-British sentiment was spreading in the colonies, and certain landlords who had a lot to lose if America gained independence, were seen as enemies by some of the landless residents of Dutchess County. In the aftermath of the nationwide stamp-act riots, a group of dissatisfied tenants began to agitate for lower rents and longer leases. Some of them had purchased land from the Indians which now was being claimed by the owners of the Philipse and Beekman patents. When they tried to retain title to their property, a skirmish broke out, in which one British soldier was killed. William Prendergast, a leader of the "rioters", was sentenced to hang, but later acquitted, and little relief was granted to the tenants.[5] But nine years later, a larger group of similar mind-ed Americans, beginning at Lexington and Concord, would give the boot to the British landlords.

DAWNING OF A NEW AGE

As soon as it became clear that the new government of the United States of America was going to last a while, a golden age of agriculture dawned in Dutchess County. Forests were cleared, stone fences crisscrossed the land, villages sprang up. Population surged, to 40,000 by 1790;[6] many of the new residents were farmers fleeing the rocky impoverished soil of New England.

The big cash crop on these early farms was wheat, which brought up to $2.75 per bushel in New York City. Corn was planted on newly-cleared land, and the "kitchen gardens" of the time in-cluded asparagus, apples (grown mostly for making hard cider), peaches, pears, quinces and currants.[7]

WESTWARD HO

Intensive agriculture in the early 19th century led to the gradual decline in soil quality referred to in Roosevelt's "tale." The midge and the Hessian fly almost wiped out the wheat crop in the 1830's. But it was, ironically, the life-long ambition of Dutchess County's own De Witt Clinton that dealt the biggest blow to the county's agriculture. When the Erie Canal, "Clinton's ditch," opened in 1825, the westward expansion that had benefitted the Hudson Valley a generation earlier moved farther west into Genessee country, open-ing vast fertile lands, and eventually driving the price of wheat below a dollar per bushel.[8]

But Dutchess County farmers adapted to the changing environ-ment, substituting rye and oats, and later hay and corn, as their main cash crops. Dairying and shepherding (there were 200,000 sheep in the county by 1840)[9] were wide-spread in the 19th century. Gail Borden's evaporated milk was produced at factories in Wassaic and elsewhere, giving a big boost to dairy production, and by 1954, almost half the county's farms were dairies.[10]

The Dutchess County Fair at Washington Hollow awarded prizes for the following vegetables in 1844: wheat, oats, corn, potatoes, sugar beets, rutabagas, carrots, clover seed, and timothy seed. Successful fruit and vegetable farmers of the 19th century in-cluded William Shook (4,000 peach trees in Red Hook), Leonard V.

Pierce (Beekman grape specialist), George J. Amato (the first of many market gardeners of Italian descent), David Haggerty and later William and George Saltford (acres of greenhouse), Joseph Bates (4,000 acres of potatoes) and even a tobacco grower, Daniel Washburn. [11]

AN EARLY FARMER SPEAKS

This excerpt from the diary of Edmund H. Hart, who had just returned from the Civil War to his family's farm on Overlook Road, gives a glimpse at farm life in the summer of 1865:

June 24th 1865—

...As Mr. Gidley was standing on the stoop yesterday he thus soliloquized "well, if I was the owner of this farm, I declare I should hardly know what to do first. There is the corn—and the potatoes to be plowed and hoed,—strawberries and cherries to be picked and nursery and garden to be cleaned of weeds, and two meadows most ready to be cut and the wheat coming on, everything seem to need doing all at once." Mr. Gidley was right, there is so much to do that I hardly dare to look forward to the finishing up of anything but yet somehow or other by our limited efforts I suppose they will be done. A good many farmers will begin haying next week. The season is much earlier than common. For instance the black cherries are just about gone and some years they last till the fourth of July. The wheat too is changing from green to bright yellow and soon the cradlers will go into it full swing."[12]

CHANGING TIMES

The Hart farm was purchased in 1838, where the first tree nursery in Dutchess County was planted, and has been in continuous operation ever since. In 1943, 100,000 bushels of apples were harvested from 375 acres cultivated by Mr. Hart's decendants, E. Stuart Hubbard Sr. and Jr.

Today farmers are finding it hard to compete with industry for good workers, and suburban sprawl is pushing land values to the point where it no longer makes economic sense to farm. Yet agriculture remains a major force in Dutchess County, with more than 600 farms producing 42 million dollars worth of crops and animal products annually.[13]

HISTORY OF ORNAMENTAL HORTICULTURE

The same national confidence that ushered in the glory years of agriculture after the enactment of the United States constitution gave rise to a renaissance in ornamental horticulture and landscape design, in which Dutchess County played a pivotal role.

The large Hudson River estates, with their wealthy and, in many cases, enlightened, owners, were perfect breeding ground for a new art form that was sweeping post-colonial America: the "natural" landscape.

ROMANTIC NOTIONS

The "natural" landscape movement was a child of the romantic era, which swept the new nation with its "modern" art, architechture, literature and poetry during the first half of the 19th century. The romantics denounced the neo-classical architecture and formal landscape design of the pre-revolutionary European society (typified by the palace of Versailles and its formal gardens of clipped hedges and symmetrical walkways). Their heroes were the poets Keats and Coleridge, authors Poe and Irving (and Shakespeare), Hudson River painters Washington Allston and Thomas Cole, statesman Andrew Jackson, and the landscape architects Humphrey Repton and Andre Parmentier, who emigrated to Brooklyn in 1824, where he started a nursery and drew the plans for at least one Hudson River estate.[14]

THE BARDS OF HYDE PARK

Dr. Samuel Bard was probably the first Dutchess County resident to promote the principles of natural landscaping. While studying in Edinburgh in 1764, Bard wrote his father, who had just taken possession of his family's estate, "Hyde Park", with a description of the way he felt the grounds should be layed out:

I think straight lines should be particularly avoided, except where they serve to lead the eye to some distant and beautiful object--serpentine walks are much more agreeable. Another object deserving of attention seems to be, to place the most beautiful and striking objects, such as water, if possible, a handsome green-house, a grove of flowering shrubs, or a remarkably fine tree in such situations that from the house they may almost all

*be seen; but to a person walking, they should be artfully
concealed until he suddenly and unexpectedly comes
upon them; so that by the surprise the pleasure may be increased: and if possible I would contrive them so that
they should contrast each other, which again greatly increases their beauty.*[15]

As it turned out, "Hyde Park" was to become one of the finest specimens of the natural style of landscape gardening in America. And Dr. Sam Bard, assisted by his father, was destined to save President George Washington's life through his skill at surgery. In 1806, Dr. Bard was chosen as the first president of the Dutchess County Agricultural Society.

The garden design work started by Dr. Bard was carried out by his colleague Dr. David Hosack, botany professor at Kings (later Columbia) College, who moved to Hyde Park in 1827. Many of the trees still flourishing at Hyde Park, which is the present-day Vander-bilt Historic Site, were planted by Dr. Hosack with design assistance from Andre Parmentier. (Unfortunately, Dr. Hosack's big chance to change history by surgery failed. His patient Alexander Hamilton perished after a duel with Aaron Burr).

EARLY GARDENERS

Another early (c. 1810) natural lanscaper was Colonal Andree De Veaux, an eccentric loyalist who contrived vistas, or views opening onto the Hudson River, at his estate near Cruger's Island. He also kept a pet kangaroo.[16] Daniel Verplanck, descendent of the Fishkill fur trader, laid out a six-acre garden around the family homestead in 1804, containing peonies, fraxinella, lemon lilies, roses and breeder tulips. For many years this garden was tended by a freed slave nam-ed James Brown, who kept a meticulous diary of daily events:

*May 3, 1829: Took a walk in the woods this day and found
a very pretty bunch of water flowers; brought them home
and gave them a place in the flower garden among the
wild plants of the collections.*[17]

DOWNING SPURS THEM ON

"Natural" landscaping was all the rage when Andrew Jackson Downing, a 26 year-old Newburgh nurseryman, published his definitive Treatise on the *"Theory and Practice of Landscape*

Gardening (1841)." Downing collected, condensed, defined and disseminated the theory behind natural landscaping, and his book had a tremendous nationwide impact; most of the landscape we see today can be traced to Downing's writings and his examples.

Downing on landscape design:

> *It is an art which selects from natural materials that abound in any country its best sylvan features, and by giving them a better opportunity than they could otherwise obtain, brings about a higher beauty of development and a more perfect expression than nature herself does.*[18]

Downing designed several estates in Dutchess County, including Blithewood, at Barrytown, and Springside, the former Matthew Vassar property on Academy Street, Poughkeepsie. He was granted commissions to design the grounds of the White House and the U.S. Capitol, and he lobbied for creation of a central park in New York City, but a tragic steamboat fire on the Hudson suddenly ended his life.

WODENETHE

Among Downing's disciples, many of whom continued his work, was Henry Winthrop Sargent, a "retired" (at age 31) lawyer from Boston and New York City who purchased a 22-acre estate on the Hudson just south of present-day Beacon. He named his estate "Wodenethe" (woody promentory) and devoted the rest of his life to landscaping it in the natural style. Sargent made extensive use of vistas, "framed" by groups of trees planted in strategic locations. (Since Wodenethe was already overgrown, many of the vistas were created by cutting away trees).[19] Windows were rearranged so that the vistas were fully visible from inside the house, appearing as living versions of a Thomas Cole painting.

By 1870, Wodenethe had become "the Most Artistic 20-Acre Place in America,"[20] visited by thousands of builders and landscape architects. Sargent used his estate as a testing ground for hundreds of unusual varieties of trees and shrubs, most of which failed to survive. He also did extensive landscape work on his neighbor's (General Joseph Howland) property "Tioronda." Wodenethe and Tioronda were eventually purchased by Craig House Hospital, where many of Sargent's most beloved specimens still flourish, including a Ginko, several larches, a gigantic weeping beech to the northwest of the hospital, and possibly the oldest living example of *Sargent's weeping hemlock.* At nearby St. Luke's Church, where Sargent was buried in 1882, stands a magnificent cut-leaf beech, of which Sargent wrote, "we hardly know a prettier or more attractive tree."[21]

BEAUTIFUL DUTCHESS

The gardeners of other Hudson River estates were laying out their grounds, some in the natural style, throughout the 19th and into the 20th century. Downing gives special praise to the several estates of Livingston family members near Barrytown, which "owe almost their entire beauty to nature." William B. Dinsmore's "the Locusts," near Staatsburgh, became a showplace and model farm during the 1880's, with 1,000 feet of greenhouses containing roses, orchids, tropical palms, and a large selection of bedding-out plants. With the help of head gardener M.J. Lynch, the Locusts also became a model farm, growing corn, oats, rye, potatoes and Jersey cattle.[22]

Walter Langdon acquired the Bards' Hyde Park estate and added a walled Italian Garden, which was enlarged and improved by Frederick W. Vanderbilt after he bought the property in 1895. This Italian Garden is presently being restored to its former state of beauty.

More recently, College Hill Park was restored by superintendant Frank M. Berry, and an extensive rock garden was transplanted there in 1931,[23] the life's work of amateur horticulturalist Clarence Lown of Forbus Street, Poughkeepsie (the rock garden is now sadly neglected). Sven M. Sward, horticulturalist and superintendant of grounds at Vassar College until his death in 1975, taught generations of students how to tend the growing things on campus, and he supervised the planting of class trees, some of which date back to the 1860's. The modern estate of Chauncey Stillman (Weathersfield), and Thorndale in Millbrook are examples of the many fine homes and parks which have continued the tradition of the landscape pioneers of Dutchess County.

NOTES

1. Nixon, Edgar B., ed.; *Franklin D. Roosevelt and Conservation;* Washington, D.C.; 1957; Vol. II, p. 11.

2. McCracken, H.N.; *Old Dutchess Forever!;* New York; 1956; p. 331.

3. McCracken, H.N.; *op. cit.;* p.43.

4. Hedrick, U.P.; *A History of Agriculture in the State of New York;* Albany, N.Y.; 1933; p. 89.

5. McCracken, H.N.; *op. cit.;* p. 312.

6. Hasbrouk, Frank, ed.;*The History of Dutchess County, New York;* Poughkeepsie, N.Y.; 1909; p. 55.

7. Mc Cracken, H.N.; *op. cit.;* p. 215.

8. Hendrick, U.P.; *op. cit.;* p. 266.

9. McCracken, H.N.; *Blithe Dutchess;* New York; 1958; p. 132.

10. *Ibid.;* p. 147.

11. *Commemorative Biographical Record of Dutchess County, N.Y.;* Chicago, Ill.; 1897.

12. Hart, Edmund H.; diary.

13. Dutchess County Cooperative Extension.

14. Spingarn, Joel E.; "Address made at the Annual Pilgrimage"; *Year Book of the Dutchess County Historical Society;* 1937; p. 40.

15. Langstaff, John B.; *Dr. Bard of Hyde Park;* New York; 1942; pp. 228-229.

16. Spingarn, Joel E.; *op. cit.;* p. 39.

17. Spingarn, Joel E.; *op. cit.;* p. 64.

18. Curtis, George W., ed.; *Rural Essays;* New York; 1856.

19. Spingarn, Joel E.; *op. cit.;* p. 56.

20. Miller, Wilhelm; "The Most Artistic 20 Acre Place in America"; *Country Life in America;* Sept. 1, 1912; p. 19.

21. Downing, A.J.; *Treatise on the Theory and Practise of Landscape Gardening;* appendix to 6th edition; New York; 1859.

22. Smith, James H.; *History of Dutchess County, New York;* Syracuse, N.Y.; 1882; pp. 310-311.

23. Poucher, J.W.; *Year Book of the Dutchess County Historical Society;* 1937; p. 105.

From an engraving in Smith's History of Dutchess County

THE DINSMORE ESTATE ca. 1885

2

Soil and Climate

By Joann Gruttadaurio and Mark Adams

Dutchess County, covering a land area of 816 square miles, is situated in southeastern New York State, between the Hudson River and the state of Connecticut. The county possesses an uneven or diversified surface and does not have large level areas. Hills and ridges of varying elevations are common; some are more than 1,000 feet in height (Brace Mountain near the northeast corner of the county, 2,340 feet above sea level, is the highest point in Dutchess County), and cut by a number of troughlike valleys.

SOIL TYPES

The soils of Dutchess County are comparatively young, and their characteristics are strongly influenced by the kind of material from which they were derived. This material was accumlated largely by glacial action.

Most of the upland is covered by ground-up rock, which was pulverized by the crushing action of millions of tons of ice as the glacier melted; it is a mixture of fine and large pieces of rock, with no evidence of sorting. The value of this "glacial till" as a source of plant nutrients is strongly influenced by the kind of rock from which it came:

• Soils from schist — occur in the eastern part of the county, mainly on the tops and slopes of Quaker Hill and Chestnut Ridge. They occupy about 6½% of the county. The low plant nutrient content of the schist rock is reflected in the soils, which generally need applications of lime and complete fertilizer.

• Soils from granite and gneiss — occur on the Housatonic highlands in the eastern part of the county, on the Hudson highlands in the southern part, and on Stissing Mountain in the north central part. The parent material contains a high proportion of quartz and relatively less of minerals bearing plant nutrients. The resultant soils are correspondingly acid and low in fertility.

• Soils from acid shale and slate — occupy a broad band extending through the central part of the county from the Columbia County line to Fishkill Creek. They occupy about 29% of the county. These soils are moderately to strongly acid and low in plant nutrients. Textures are commonly silt loam, or slightly heavier than those of the soils derived from granite and gneiss, and the capacity to hold water and plant nutrients is correspondingly greater.

• Soils from calcareous sandstone and slate — occupy a broad belt in the western part of the county. They lie east of the area occupied by slate and shale and cover about 20% of the county. In physical characteristics they are similar to comparable soils derived from acid shale and slate, but they contain much more lime and presumably more of other plant nutrients, so they are considered more fertile. The deep subsoils are slightly acid or neutral, and the surface soils are moderately acid.

• Soils from limestone and slate — these very deep well-drained soils occur in scattered areas throughout the eastern half of the county in association with soils of the acid shale and slate group and of the limestone group. The limestone is sufficient to make them neutral or calcareous in the lower subsoil.

• Soils from limestone — have developed from glacial till in which the principal rock material is limestone. These soils generally have a calcareous subsoil, though the plowed layer may be slightly to moderately acid. They are darker in color than soils derived from till that contains less lime.

Although the abovementioned soils derived from glacial till are the most abundant soil types in the county, other categories are represented:

• Soils derived from glacial outwash — water from the melting glacier flowed out in torrents southward along natural valleys, carrying with it huge quantities of ground-up and broken rock. As the speed of the waters slackened, these materials were deposited in layers. The heavier pieces were deposited first and gave rise to deposits of layered sand and gravel, called glacial outwash. This is the parent material of the highly productive nearly level soils that occupy much of the valleys.

• Lake-laid sediments — in places near the Hudson River were lakes into which fine material was washed. This material settled as layers of silt, clay, and fine sand.

• Recent alluvium — the present streams carry sediments, and through the centuries they have laid these down on the first bottoms during floods.

• Muck — plants and water-loving animals have died and settled to the bottom of ponds at spots throughout the county to develop into organic soils. The largest area of muck soil occurs along the swamp river in the southeastern part of the county. If it can be adequately drained, muckland is the most productive soil type for vegetable production.

The soils of Dutchess County differ greatly in characteristics and suitability for use. Silt loam textures predominate, although texture of most soil types varies from gravelly sandy loam to silty clay loam. Generally several associated soils occur in complex patterns, making it difficult to present an accurate map of the general types found in Dutchess County. A soil survey of Dutchess County was completed in 1955 by the U.S. Department of Agriculture, and is now in the process of being revised. Copies of the survey, from which most of the information presented in this chapter was lifted, and detailed maps of soil types, can be obtained at the Dutchess County Soil Conservation Service, at the Farm and Home Center in Millbrook.

SOIL TESTING

Soils in Dutchess County tend to be acidic, necessitating the addition of limestone for many crops to grow properly.

The Dutchess County Cooperative Extension offers a soil testing service, to test for soil pH (acidity) and available nutrients (phosphorus, potassium, magnesium and calcium). The soil to be

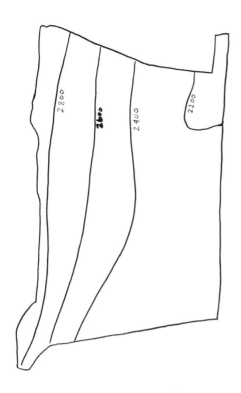

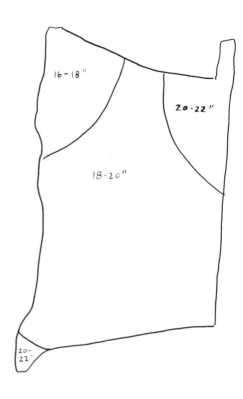

Dutchess County accumulative growing degree days, freeze-free season; base 50°. Growing degree days relate plant growth to air temperature. The number on the map is derived by totalling the average daily temperatures above 50°.

$(\frac{max - min}{2} - 50°)$ for each day during the freeze-free period.

Source: Dept. of Agronomy, Cornell University

Dutchess County Average Total Precipitation
May to September

Source: Dept. of Agronomy, Cornell University

SOILS MAP FOR DUTCHESS COUNTY

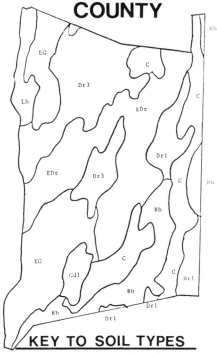

KEY TO SOIL TYPES

C = Nellis areas; are deep soils, high lime

Drl = Hollis areas; are shallow, gently sloping, well-drained, low lime with low water capacity and moderate permeability.

Dr3 = Nassau areas; are rolling, contain acid soils, that are shallow to bedrock, have a low water capacity and moderate permeability.

EDr = Bernardston — Nassau areas;

EG = Bernardston — Hoosic areas;

Gd1 = Alton — Hoosic areas; can be nearly level, rolling or hilly, well drained, require lime, have a moderate water capacity and quite permeable.

Lh = Hudson area; are deep soils formed from clay lake deposits, medium to high lime, with a high water capacity but slow permeability.

Rh = Rock outlays areas; have exposed rock outcrop or bedrock not capable of supporting plant life and limit the usefulness.

tested should be taken from several locations within the test area, six inches below the surface. Thoroughly mix and dry the final sample, which should consist of a total of one cup of soil, and place it in a clean plastic container. There is a fee for this service.

CLIMATE

Everyone loves to talk about the weather, because there's so little that can be done about it. It seems that no matter where you go, someone is always willing to comment that it's been either too hot, too cold, too windy, wet, sunny or even too nice! But all in all, Dutchess County seems to boast some of the best weather anywhere.

Officially, the mid-Hudson region has a humid continental climate. On the hardiness maps in most gardening books, Dutchess County is in "zone 6", where the average minimum winter temperature is -10° to 0°. This zone stretches in a wide band from central New Mexico across the Texas panhandle, southern Missouri, Illinois, Indiana and Ohio, and heads northeast across Pennsylvania into northern New Jersey, where it intersects Dutchess County. From here, zone 6 reaches through Connecticut, Rhode Island and up along the coast of Massachusettes and Southern Maine. Theoretically, garden plants which are hardy in zone 6 can be grown in this area. In reality, of course, the climates within zone 6 show wide variations, and the temperature extremes are more pronounced in one section (the mountains of West Virginia) than in another (Rhode Island). Even within Dutchess County, the temperature in both mean and extreme, can vary considerably. The Hudson River has a moderating influence on our climate, and the communities closest to the river will experience a smaller variation from the average temperature than will those in the outlying areas. Northern areas of the county, as would be expected, and especially northeastern areas, tend to be cooler than southwestern areas of the county, although I have noticed many mornings when Poughkeepsie has been colder than either Kingston or Albany far to the north.

Let's discuss the climate of Dutchess County as it relates to the farmer or gardener. (I have gathered the pertinent data from my own records and from the NOAA weather station at the Dutchess County Airport):

GROWING SEASON

The average freeze-free period is 153 days; from May 5 to October 6. That is, tender annual flowers and vegetables plants can be set out on May 5, and they have a 50-50 chance of escaping a damaging frost. The probability of frost is only 10% if they are planted after May 17th. I've kept my own records and have seen the following variations in the final frost date at Poughkeepsie:

1980	May 10
1981	May 20
1982	April 23
1983	May 18
1984	May 19
1985	May 9
1986	May 10

Tender plants set out prior to the last frost date can be protected with newspaper, burlap or similar covering. Late spring freezes occur on calm, clear nights. My recollection of the latest spring frost was on June 3, 1986, but it was so light as to cause no significant damage to Dutchess County crops.

The first fall frost, which can damage unharvested vegetables and blacken exposed foliage on annual flowers, occurs on the average October 6th, although many light freezes have been seen in late September.

WINTER CHILL

The coldest temperature recorded in Dutchess County in recent memory was -30°F on January 21, 1961. As I remember, my father's peach trees in Salt Point were killed. On the average, the mercury dips below 0°F on 9 days each year.

SUMMER HEAT

Heat waves are an unfortunate part of Dutchess County's climate, but believe it or not, most garden crops, such as corn and tomatoes, thrive in very hot weather, if they are given the proper amount of water and nutrients. On July 3, 1966, a 103 degree reading (in the shade) was recorded at Dutchess County Airport, and each year, 15 days can be expected to bake in at 90° or above.

AUGUST SHOWERS

No, April is not the soggiest month in Dutchess County. August, with its frequent thunderstorms, douses us with an average 3.77 inches of rain. Our precipitation is fairly consistent throughout the summer, but most of the vegetable farmers I know in our county rely on their irrigation systems to supplement the occasional summer dry spells. We weren't worrying about irrigation in July, 1975, when a record 13 inches of rain poured down in a week. Our field of peppers, underwater for 2 days, was a total loss.

SNOW

43 inches of snow can be expected to fall each winter season. Naturally, snow is the gardener's delight, as it protects plants from severe winter winds. Incidentally, I've found that the ground can be worked most years into the early part of December, before a permanent freeze sets in, which thaws out in late March or early April.

EARLY THAWS

An occasional February thaw, accompanied by up to 70° temperatures, blazing sun and warm winds, can wreak havoc on exposed vegetation. Evergreens, azaleas, roses and perennials will lose the moisture from their leaves, and their still frozen roots will be unable to replace it. Plantings on the south side of buildings might begin to sprout, only to be frozen back when cold weather returns. These pre-spring thaws, typical in Dutchess County, are the reason exposed plantings must be protected with burlap or other winter coverings.

HAIL

Fortunately, hail is infrequent in the Hudson Valley. A severe hailstorm some 35 years ago wiped out dozens of greenhouse operations throughout the county, and over the last several years the apple harvest has fallen victim to an occasional hailstorm. Hail is localized, so precise statistics are unavailable. Poughkeepsie and New Paltz got clobbered by marble-sized hail on May 31, 1986, but Rhinebeck and Millbrook were spared.

DUTCHESS COUNTY TEMPERATURE AND PRECIPITATION DATA

TEMPERATURE (F)

	MEANS			EXTREMES						MEAN NUMBER OF DAYS			
										MAX		MIN	
	DAILY MAXIMUM*	DAILY MINIMUM*	MONTHLY*	RECORD HIGHEST	YEAR	DAY	RECORD LOWEST	YEAR	DAY	90 AND ABOVE	32 AND BELOW	32 AND BELOW	0 AND BELOW
JAN	34.0	14.8	24.4	63+	75	11	-30	61	21	0	13	29	4
FEB	36.9	16.6	26.8	72+	54	16	-23+	67	8	0	9	26	3
MAR	46.1	26.3	36.2	84+	77	30	-13+	67	19	0	2	24	0
APR	59.7	36.2	48.0	94+	76	18	13	54	3	0	0	11	0
MAY	70.5	46.0	58.3	96+	69	29	27+	63	24	1	0	2	0
JUN	79.2	55.6	67.5	99+	64	30	36+	64	3	3	0	0	0
JUL	84.1	60.5	72.4	103+	66	3	43+	57	3	6	0	0	0
AUG	82.1	59.1	70.6	100+	55	5	38+	65	31	4	0	0	0
SEP	74.3	51.0	62.7	101+	53	2	26+	63	24	1	0	1	0
OCT	63.4	39.5	51.5	88	63	7	18+	74	20	0	0	8	0
NOV	50.6	31.2	40.9	78+	74	1	11+	72	23	0	0	18	0
DEC	38.2	20.3	29.3	66+	79	12	-13+	80	26	0	8	27	2
YEAR	59.9	38.1	49.1	103	JUL 66	3	-30	JAN 61	21	15	32	146	9

PRECIPITATION TOTALS (INCHES)

	MEAN*	GREATEST MONTHLY*	YEAR	GREATEST DAILY	YEAR	DAY	SNOW MEAN	SNOW MAXIMUM MONTHLY	SNOW YEAR	.10 OR MORE	.50 OR MORE	1.00 OR MORE
JAN	2.75	8.73	78	2.02	79	21	10.9	30.8	78	6	1	0
FEB	2.42	5.20	62	1.52	77	24	10.8	31.0	67	5	2	0
MAR	3.28	6.63	53	2.22	77	22	8.3	34.6	67	7	2	1
APR	3.66	7.41	52	2.51	70	02	1.5	19.6	61	7	3	1
MAY	3.62	7.74	72	2.80	68	29	.1	4.0	77	7	2	1
JUN	3.43	7.99	72	2.84	73	29	.0	.0		6	2	1
JUL	3.50	13.63	75	4.72	75	14	.0	.0		6	2	1
AUG	3.77	12.71	55	4.02	71	28	.0	.0		5	2	1
SEP	3.66	7.94	77	3.77	66	21	.0	.0		5	2	1
OCT	3.30	10.40	55	4.48	55	15	.0	.6	62	5	2	1
NOV	3.57	8.11	72	2.18	69	05	1.7	8.2	68	6	2	1
DEC	3.20	8.65	73	2.39	52	11	9.3	31.0	69	6	2	1
YEAR	40.16	13.63	JUL 75	4.72	JUL 75	14	42.6	34.6	MAR 67	71	24	10

*FROM 1951-80 NORMALS   + ALSO ON EARLIER DATES.

3

Let's Grow Annual Flowers

By Ruth Link

The arrival of the seed catalog coincides with the darkest days of winter when our spirits are apt to be at low ebb. Aglow as these catalogs are with splashes of vibrant color, they invite our anticipation of spring with dreams of growing the most beautiful garden ever. Not an impossible dream if we make generous use of annuals.

The botanical definition of an annual is a plant which grows from seed, produces flowers, matures its seed and dies in one season. To the gardener it is any plant, sown in spring, which will produce summer or fall blossoms and not live over winter. In Dutchess County's climate this includes plants such as petunias, pansies and coleus which are perennials in their native countries or in warmer areas, but which are too tender to survive our winters.

ANNUALS FOR COLOR

Annuals are divided into three categories. Hardy annuals can take light frost without being killed or badly damaged. Therefore seeds can be planted outdoors a couple of weeks before the last frost is expected. These include sweet peas, alyssum, snapdragons and calendulas. Half hardy annuals can tolerate long periods of dampness and cold, but are damaged or killed by frost and therefore their seeds should not be sown until preferably a week after the date for the last possible frost as some require fairly warm soil to germinate. The tender annuals such as marigolds, petunias and zinnias must have warm soil to germinate. It becomes evident that it is important to know the date of the last frost in spring. This is usually considered to be May 10th in Dutchess County. You also need to know the date of the first frost in fall (about October 1st) and the length of time required for the annuals of your choice to mature and bloom. Bear in mind, however, that there are differences even within the county. Our gardening friends in the eastern and northern parts of the county will be quick to tell you that they have frost as late as May 31st and as early as the second or third week in September. In the more central areas and particularly close to the Hudson River (a moderating influence) the last frost may be slightly earlier than May 10th, though on very rare occasions it has been as late as May 31st. The first fall frost along the river often does not come until mid October and has been as late as November 4th.

It would be good to mention here that some plants which are actually biennials are often treated as annuals in Dutchess County. A bedding plant grower might start these well in advance, the gardener buy and plant them, and they will come to bloom the same season in which they are planted. A biennial, however, is actually a plant which germinates and grows the first year, but flowers and comes to seed the second year. Some of these are very showy and easy to grow. They include sweet william, canterbury bells, foxglove, hollyhock and pansies.

WHY ANNUALS?

Having defined what an annual is, let's consider some of the good reasons for growing these flowers. First of all, they are rewarding for beginning gardeners, since they are quite willing to grow without the need for special equipment or a high degree of maintenance. They are probably the least expensive plant material. A new garden can be grown very quickly using all annuals or they can fill in temporarily while a more permanent and slower growing planting is getting started. Incorporated in a perennial bed, they will provide color after early blooming perennials have faded and before the fall blooming ones start. In fact, many annuals bloom continuously through the summer until frost. They supply lovely accents as edgings for shrubs, under trees, and in containers. They come in a wide range of color and height and their temporary nature allows one to try a whole new scheme every year. Last, but not least, so many of them, like sweet peas, asters, calendulas, larkspur, marigolds, snapdragons and zinnias, provide long lasting cut flowers.

We have discussed the frost dates in relation to the planting of seeds. Actually, many people find it more satisfactory to set out bedding plants. Timing for these is also dependent on the last date for frost as the tender annual plants cannot be set out prior to that date. You will often see bedding plants for sale early in the spring. Don't be tempted to buy the tender annuals. Wait for that last frost date. Hardy annuals, of course, can go in sooner. There are advantages to growing annuals from seed as well as to using bedding plants. We may decide we want to grow something special for which bedding plants are not readily available locally. For seeds which germinate easily when direct sown into the garden space where they are expected to grow, there is also the advantage of less handling and, therefore, the absence of shock in transplanting which sets the plant back. Direct sowing, however, is only advisable for larger seeds of faster maturing plants. One must expect a larger loss of these seedlings to weather, insects and animals and a germination rate of only about 60%.

Bedding plants, while more expensive than seeds, are readily available in a fairly wide variety and present distinct advantages. The first is that they enable the gardener to have a virtually instant garden with remarkably little effort. In addition a few seeds are difficult to handle or have special requirements for which the average gardener may lack the necessary coping skills or equipment. The begonia, for instance, has extremely fine seed, difficult to handle. A few, like geraniums, lobelia, thunbergia and vinca need higher temperatures to germinate. Some, such as begonia, petunia, ageratum and vinca are very slow growing so, in order to have blooms reasonably early, need to be started very early indoors, thus necessitating a greenhouse environment or, at least, a good lighting set-up.

A few suggestions of seed companies whose catalogs have a wide variety of quality seed suitable for our growing area as well as some good cultural information follows. There are many other seed catalogs available. Ask around among your gardening friends.

W. Atlee Burpee Co.
300 Park Ave.
Warminster, PA 18974

Park Seed Co.
Hwy 254 N.
Greenwood SC 29647-0001

Harris Seeds
Moreton Farm
3670 Buffalo Rd.
Rochester, NY 14624

Stokes Seeds, Inc.
Box 548
Buffalo, NY 14240

PLAN FIRST

The first consideration of every gardener should be planning. Location of the garden is a prime concern. Most annuals prefer an open, sunny location, but a few are best suited to shade and we will discuss some individual preferences later. You might want to have a bed of nothing but annuals in a slightly out of the way area to be used as a cutting garden. Or you may wish to combine annuals and perennials for a sequence of bloom so here you will need a flower chart found in seed catalogs like Burpee's and Park's which state the usual period of bloom. Most homes have some type of evergreen foundation planting which can benefit tremendously from an uplift of color provided by a border of bright red salvia, red geraniums, pink begonia, or golden marigolds for instance. Don't neglect the area around the base of trees which can be brightened by impatiens or begonias in various colors. Finally, consider the use of hanging baskets at your front door or along your porch. Containers can be grouped at corners of a terrace or next to an entrance. Window boxes can be used along a south or west facing porch for quick growing morning glory vines which will provide shade in short order as they climb strings to the porch roof. Annuals take very well to these containers with proper care.

3-1 Petunia —
Dutchess County's favorite sunny annual.

In addition to location, it is a good idea to consider color. You may want a specific color scheme or just a riot of many colors. Do bear in mind the background color, however, and take into consideration that dark colors recede into the background; bright, light colors will overwhelm dark colors; dark blues will be lost against dark green evergreens and some shades of pink and red will clash with the off reds or slightly blue color of some brick walls.

PREPARATION

Having made our plans, the next step is to prepare the soil in the flower bed. It is important to wait until the soil has lost excess moisture before starting to work. This won't be until late March or well into April depending on location. Test for moisture by scooping up a handful of soil and squeezing it lightly. If it crumbles apart fairly easily, it is ready. Working soil which still contains too much moisture will result in hard, dry clods later on. Dutchess soil tends to be heavy and on the clay side, although some areas, especially in Eastern Dutchess have a somewhat gravelly content. Most annuals like a well drained soil so it is strongly recommended that you amend your soil with organic material. This can come from your compost pile, leaf mold or well rotted manure. Spread about two inches over the bed and spade to a depth of six to eight inches. Next add some fertilizer. Use an inorganic fertilizer in the 5-10-5 or 5-10-10 ratio, spread at a rate of about three pounds per 100 square feet. Organic gardeners can use their favorite organic fertilizer. Rake this in. Annuals grow best at a pH of 6.5 to 6.8. For a very nominal fee you can have the pH tested at the Dutchess County Cooperative Extension Service in Millbrook where they will give you recommendations for raising or lowering the pH if necessary.

PLANTING

If you are planning to direct sow seed, first be sure the soil temperature is warm enough to allow germination. Water the soil well the day before. Sow the seeds according to the directions on the packet in drills or broadcast. In general, seeds are covered with soil to a depth of three to four times their diameter. Keep the seed bed moist using the finest spray of your hose nozzle. Once sprouted, young seedlings need daily watering in sunny weather. Take care not to wash them away. A perforated hose is ideal for this purpose. The bed should receive an inch of water per week in cool weather and from one and a half to two inches in warm weather. This applies to bedding plants as well. Thin seedlings with scissors to avoid disturbing the roots of the plants to be left. It is important to give each plant enough space to grow and thrive. Space requirements are usually recommended on seed packets, but you may place them a little closer for a bush effect. If crowded too close, however, they will compete for sun, root space, nutrients and water and the result will be spindly plants with fewer flowers.

If you decide to go the bedding plant route, first try to estimate your needs before buying plants. Look for younger plants without blooms and with compact foliage and good, green leaf color. The sooner you plant after purchasing the better. Try to pick a cloudy, cool day after a good rain. Barring that, opt for late afternoon. Water the plants in their nursery pack before beginning the planting. If you cannot plant immediately after purchase, be sure to water them daily. They may even need it twice a day. Keep them in their containers in a lightly shaded area. When planting, dig a hole a little larger than the plant's root ball. Ease the plant out of the container by pushing it up from the bottom if in individual type packs. If not in this type pack remove the entire group of plants in a block and pull them gently apart. It is best to remove and plant only one plant at a time so that the roots do not dry out. We like to fill the hole with a half strength liquid fertilizer before setting the plant in. Place plant at the same level it was grown in the container, fill in with soil and firm slightly. Give it some more water now. If your plants are in peat pots, tear off the top edge of the pot. It acts as a wick allowing moisture to be drawn out of the soil. Also break away the bottom to allow roots free access to the soil. See that the peat pot is well covered with soil. If it is very hot and sunny for a day or two after planting, rig up something to shade the plants.

GROWING THEM ON

Now all that is needed is a little tender, loving care to insure success. It is a good idea to mulch. This conserves water, cuts down weeding, improves the soil structure and helps maintain an even soil temperature. Good organic mulches are composted leaves, shredded bark or wood chips. These should be two inches deep. Or you may use black plastic and set your plants through holes in the plastic. This looks tacky unless covered with a thin layer of wood chips or bark. Next take any flowers off newly planted bedding plants. It hurts, but do it anyway. Pinching out the growing tips will help to make the plant bushy. As the plants grow, stake the tall ones so they don't fall over. By all means take off the faded flowers regularly - every other day at least. This is called dead heading and it insures continued blooms. The plant's goal is to set seed for the next generation and it will keep blooming in an effort to do so if you keep preventing seeds from maturing. Otherwise its energy goes to producing seeds, not flowers. Incidentally, if you didn't mulch, you must weed!

You fertilized your soil before planting, your plants were set out in mid May and have been growing for two months. They will have another two or three months to grow before frost. They are probably getting a little hungry. Another pound of 5-10-5 or 5-10-10 per 100 square feet applied now in mid July will help them to continue on at their best. Also inspect them regularly for signs of trouble. Ragged leaves with holes indicate beetles or caterpillars. Sometimes tiny, sucking creatures known as aphids can be seen covering the stem or whole plants may be demolished by slugs. Dealing with these is covered in another chapter. On the whole annuals are among the most trouble free plants.

GARDENING IN CONTAINERS

If you choose to plant in containers, use a packaged soil or a mix of one half garden soil and one half peat moss or compost. You might add some perlite to this. It is best to have drainage holes in the bottom of the container. If you have a favorite pot without holes, consider setting another clay pot inside it or at least put an inch of stones or pebbles in the bottom. Choose long blooming plants of a compact nature and combine several forms in one pot. Crowd these plants a little closer together than in the garden and compensate by watering and feeding them more often. They will need daily water and one half strength liquid fertilizer every two weeks. Be sure to pinch off dead flowers and be careful not to let water accumulate in the bottom of the pot.

SHADE LOVERS

When it comes to some of our own favorites, we would have to mention a couple of shade lovers. Impatiens is truly rewarding planted around the base of a tree or in a shady corner. It needs to be started early indoors. Grow it in reasonably fertile soil and keep it moist and it will bloom profusely right up to frost. It comes in a variety of pink, red, orange, fuschia and white and in varying heights from four to twenty-four inches. There is also a new variety called gem which will withstand sun.

3-2 Impatiens —
Dutchess County's favorite shady annual.

Fibrous rooted begonias are also happy in light shade, although they will tolerate almost any light conditions and will also bloom continuously. They withstand the elements and are not bothered by pests. These, too, must be sown indoors very early and therefore we prefer to use bedding plants. Their usual height is six to twelve inches depending on variety. Allow the soil to dry out between waterings. They are especially nice for borders and edgings and may be dug up in fall and brought indoors where they will continue to bloom most of the winter if you pinch them back.

Coleus comes in many shades of pink, red, green and yellow and many leaf forms. It is grown for its foliage. It will grow in sun, but is at its best in filtered shade. Keep it moist and pinch back all flowers. Pruning the stems somewhat will deep it bushy. A large pot or urn planted with a variety of color and leaf forms presents a striking appearance at an entrance or along the edge of a terrace. These are fairly easy to grow from seed.

3-3 Lobelia —
Increasingly popular for shady areas.

SUN LOVERS

Petunias are favorites everywhere. They come in a very wide range of color and flower form and size. This is another plant which needs an early start and is a little tricky to germinate so we recommend bedding plants. Petunias like well drained soil and full sun. Be sure to pinch the growing tips back when you set them out and again after they have their first flush of flowers as they tend to get leggy. Picking the dead flowers off is a must. The cascade types are attractive in hanging containers as they spill over the edges. Water the container plants well when the soil feels dry just below the surface, but be sure that the water can drain off at the bottom. Petunias can't stand wet feet.

A plant grown for its foliage rather than its flowers, dusty miller presents an interesting counterpoint when used as an edging for a bed of flowers. We like it especially edging a bed of pink begonias. Actually a perennial, it is grown as an annual here. It likes well drained soil, high in organic material and full sun, but tolerates some shade. Water it lightly and remove any flowers. Also trim it back occasionally to maintain a compact shape.

If you have a foundation planting facing south, there is nothing like bright red salvia for an accent. Salvia comes in a few other colors too, but the red seems to be more attractive to humming birds which are such a joy to watch. Salvia needs well drained, but moist, rich soil. Keep it watered and don't forget an extra shot of fertilizer.

FLOWERS FOR CUTTING

Cosmos is perfect for the background of a flower bed since it grows tall. It does well in sandy or gravelly soil and likes full sun. Easy to grow from direct sown seed, it needs to be staked. Do not give this one extra fertilizer as it will deter flowering. This is a good flower for cutting.

While we're on the subject of good cutting flowers, don't pass by the snapdragons. They now come in all heights from six inches to four feet and a wide range of color. These are best sown indoors too if you want early bloom, otherwise they can be direct seeded when the soil temperature is about 70°. These seeds require light for germination so don't cover them. Just press lightly into soil. They like rich, well drained soil. Water them moderately and remove faded blooms. They should also be pinched to increase branching and flowering. Snapdragons self seed readily and will surprise you by popping up unexpectedly the following year. We have even found snaps in a protected location sending out shoots from the base of the previous year's plant.

Marigolds are among the easiest flowers to grow. They germinate readily, but the tall African types take time to come to flower, so should be started indoors. They like moist, well drained, rich soil and should have their faded blossoms removed regularly except for the triploid or mule type which is sterile and therefore not weakened by seed bearing. Terrific for cut flowers, but watch the slugs - they love it!

For ease in growing, zinnias match marigolds. They can be direct sown after the last frost. They also need well drained soil with a high organic content and full sun. Give these enough space so they get good air circulation and apply water at the base as they can have a problem with mildew. If this happens, use a fungicide. Pinch back for bushiness and don't hesitate to cut flowers for bouquets. Remove faded blossoms.

ROCK GARDENS

If you have a rock garden or an area where the soil is thin, sandy or gravelly and very sunny, portulaca will thrive. It grows on the worst soil, wants very little water and needs no care. It will bloom joyously in hot, sunny Dutchess summers.

Sweet William, while technically a biennial, is often treated like an annual and some recent hybrids are actually true annuals. This will grow in full sun or light shade and prefers a more neutral soil. Once started, you never need to plant it again as it self seeds very readily. To insure this you will have to leave a few flowers to mature seed at the end of its blooming period. These also provide long lasting cut flowers.

Another good cutting flower is calendula. It comes in bright yellows and orange. The flower heads have been used for flavoring soups and stews and sometimes the petals are used in salads. This can be direct sown early as it is hardy, but it takes a while to mature, so for early flowers, it should be started indoors. It can suffer from mildew, therefore water early in the day so it has a chance to dry and use a fungicide if necessary. We have not experienced this problem.

Another easy to grow annual which likes sandy, well drained soil is the nasturtium. Direct sow this and do not fertilize, but see that it has plenty of moisture. Unfortunately our summers are sometimes a bit hot so try to find a cool spot for it. Its leaves will add zip to your salads.

It would be possible to continue on with a discussion of a few dozen more varieties of annuals, but the above are favorites of ours which grow well in Dutchess. Most gardeners are adventurous and will experiment with a few new varieties each year while continuing to plant their favorites, so let's keep on growing.

4

Let's Grow Perennials

By Sandra Reilly

A perennial garden is excellent for the impatient gardener. In a few years there will be masses of color and fragrance from these fast-growing plants. Perennials emerge in the Spring and by mid-June my garden is a sea of color. To me the garden is very therapeutic. It soothes on a summer morning as I sit with my morning coffee. It can also be a way of venting frustrations as I pull weeds and prune flowers. I hope by the time you finish this chapter you will be ready to try perennials in your garden.

I was introduced to perennials by a neighbor who happened to be dividing plants in her large garden. She arrived with a wheelbarrow full of plants, some nameless, and I had to quickly find room for them. My garden was not planned, but since perennials are easily moved I have not had any problems.

Perennials are herbaceous plants that die back in the winter. Most of them do not have a very long bloom cycle, two weeks at the most. Unlike annuals, perennials come up every year and many live a very long time. Daylilies, for example, can live to be fifty years old.

PLANNING

A perennial garden that has flowers all summer takes some planning. I have prepared a chart that lists the plants I have in my garden and the season they bloom. Some of these plants overlap two seasons and these I have noted. I have also listed colors, height, and the best locations (sun or shade) to help you in planning your garden. All these plants have done well for me here in Dutchess County. They survived the winters, most with very little protection. Keep in mind that my garden is somewhat protected; if you have yours in an exposed area you may want to add more protection. I have listed the plants by their Latin names. You are sure to get the exact species you want at garden centers or through catalogs by knowing the Latin names as well as the common ones. There are many plants that have the same comon name which can make for confusion.

In planning your garden an eastern exposure is best if you have a choice. The plants receive about six hours of sun and some shade in the heat of the day. If you have shaded areas there are some perennials that do quite well and some that even require a shaded spot. I enjoy seeing my garden from the house; you too may want to locate you garden close to the living area of your home. Make the garden as large as you can manage easily. You can always add to it later if you get the "perennial bug". Try to keep the width of the garden no more than eight feet. This makes for easier weeding.

Now that you have decided where to put your garden, draw up a rough plan of the plants you would like to use. Generally tall plants are toward the back of the garden and the smaller ones up front. There are "warm" and "cool" colors, warm being the shades of red, yellow, and orange; cool ones being pink, lavender, and blue. White is a "cross-over" color, you can use it between groups of cool and warm shades. Foliage colors are also important; there are many shades of green and grey greens. One of the nicest things about planning a garden is that you can use the colors and plants you like best; then the garden becomes an expression of your own individuality.

My garden includes spring bulbs as well as perennials. If I were starting again I'm not sure I would combine the two types of plants. I'm forever digging up the bulbs by mistake and the bulb foliage is distracting as it dies back. I try to put annuals and late perennials in front of the bulbs but sometimes it's not possible. A few spring bulbs do blend well with the spring flowering perennials such as the Bleeding Heart and the Virginia Bluebells. Make sure to mark where the bulbs are planted to avoid my problem of disturbing them.

PREPARATION

In my area the soil has clay so I try to add lots of peat moss, leaf mold and compost to make the soil workable. Everytime I add a perennial to my garden I also add some peat moss or compost. I use a 5-10-5 or 5-10-10 fertilizer early in the Spring as the plants are emerging. About ½ cup dug around each plant seems to be enough. When I plant new perennials I add some superphosphate for root growth.

Established perennials can usually take some dry spells with very little damage. Newly planted ones should be kept moist for a few weeks. Ideally a soaker hose wound through the plants is the best way to water the garden. Turn the holes in the soaker down into the ground to keep the foliage dry. The plants should be thoroughly soaked not just sprinkled on the surface. Watering during the day allows the foliage to dry out before evening, cutting down on mildew and disease problems. Mulching the garden will help to conserve moisture.

MULCHING

No garden is entirely maintenance free but there are some techniques that help keep garden chores to a minimum. A six inch mulch of bark chips helps to keep the weeds down. If you have a large area to mulch this can get quite expensive. Pine needles, oak leaves or grass clippings can also be used; they may not be as attractive as the bark mulch but they will do the job. Herbicides are not a good idea in the perennial garden; any drift can damage the plants. I keep a spray bottle of Amitrol handy for the poison ivy but I spray on calm days. I would not recommend plastic mulch in the garden. Many of the plants multiply by underground roots and the plastic would hinder the emergence of side shoots. Plastic is not very attractive unless it's covered with pine chips. I probably spend on the average, three hours a week weeding my garden. I find this to be an enjoyable chore, much better than housework!

MAINTENANCE

As I weed the garden, I also "dead-head" the plants, taking off any of the flowers that are going to seed. This puts more energy into the vegetative growth. Some plants such as the biennial foxglove should be allowed to go to seed for more plants the following year. Columbine, if allowed to self seed will revert back to a "muddy" lavender.

I have some insect problems on the perennials but not usually enough to spray. I use a fungicide on the phlox and the beebalm for mildew. Since I have so many bees, birds and butterflies in my garden, I am very reluctant to use any type of chemicals.

In the winter I cover some of my plants with pine boughs (Christmas trees are good) after the first hard frost. This keeps them from heaving out of the ground. Some plants that I find need mulching are chrysanthemums, baby's breath, ballonflowers, and coral bells.

Since there is a good section in the book on annuals, I won't go into much detail on their care and selection. I find that annuals are excellent as "fillers" for bare spaces left by spring bulbs or plants such as poppies, Virginia bluebells, and bleeding heart. In my garden, I use red nicotiana, purple and red salvia, marigolds of all sizes, alyssum, cleome, cosmos, and ageratum. These give the garden color during times when the perennials are not in bloom.

One of the nicest things about a perennial garden is that you can share plants with friends. All perennials need dividing at some time and these divisions are a good way to swap plants. There are so many plants in my garden that were given to me by friends I often think of it as a "friendship garden". Perennials can be divided almost any time during the season; usually Spring is the best while the plants are small and easy to handle. If you want to move the plants around during the season be careful to keep them well watered. Try to get a good root system for each division and keep the plants moist until they can be re-planted. Try to divide on a cloudy day and shade the plants for a few days if the weather is hot.

A few of the plants on the chart are good for the beginning gardener. They are easy to grow and they have few insect and disease problems.

VARIETIES TO TRY

Astilbe Likes moist soil with some organic matter. It blooms in June and July. Astilbe do well in shade or some morning sun. The plumed flowers come in shades of pink, red and white. These plants multiply rapidly and they may be divided every three years.

Bleeding heart is a lovely plant for the Spring. It likes shade or morning sun. The tiny heart-shaped flowers come in shades of pink and white. This plant dies back in late June so you might want to plant some annuals in front to fill in the space.

Daylilies are really tough plants, you can grow them in semishade or sun. They multiply quickly and have very few insect or disease problems. Be careful where you put these plants in your garden, they can take over very quickly.

Rudbeckia is a summer plant that multiplies quickly. It needs full sun with a well-drained soil. You may have to stake it, although I grow the variety 'Goldsturm which is very compact and does not need staking. The flowers are good for cutting.

Hosta is another tough plant and an excellent one for shade. The green, yellow-green, and green and white foliage add color where the flowers cannot bloom. Some of the plants have lavender flowers that bloom in July. Deer and slugs are a problem with these plants but the hosta usually survive.

Peonies are such lovely plants that they are worth the space they require in the garden. They must be planted in the Fall. The "eye" on the division should be only two inches below the surface, any deeper and the plant may not bloom. Peonies do best in full sun with fertile soil. Add superphosphate to the hole when planting and fertilize every Spring. Once established the plants will live for years.

ROSES

I have a few rose bushes in my garden and although they are not herbaceous perennials I enjoy them as a cut flower. Roses are considered a high maintenance plant, which means they must be sprayed, fertilized, and winter protected. I use a systemic insecticide and fertilizer combination in granular form applied every six weeks and this seems to take care of most problems. In the winter, I cover the graft at the base of the plant with about six inches of soil. I then put a wire cage over the top of the plant and fill it with leaves. Most of my roses come through the winter with minimal damage. Roses should be uncovered when the forsythia blooms. Try not to prune back much of the growth in the Fall, leave some to compansate for winter damage. When a rose is cut it should be just above the first set of five leaves, This will cause a new blooming shoot to form.

ASTILBE

(Common) BLEEDING HEART

DAY LILY

RUDBECKIA

LET'S GROW

You have many choices in perennials; the ones I have listed are only a few of the many varieties available. The best way to select plants is to go to a reputable nursery or through a catalog. Try to visit perennial gardens in the area, there are some listed in this book. I use a few reference books as guides in selecting and growing perennials. These are the books I find most helpful:

Perennials — How to Select, Grow and Enjoy
Pamela Harper & John McGourty
H.P. Publishers

Successful Gardening with Perennials
Helen Van Pelt Wilson
Doubleday & Company

The Garden Book
White Flower Farm

I hope this information has been helpful in selecting and growing perennials. You will find perennials to be a great source of pleasure and satisfaction. Like all gardening there is some work involved but I think it is well worth the effort. Each Spring as my perennials begin to emerge, I enjoy them all over again. The only problem is you always want more plants. I am thinking of enlarging my garden next Spring!

PERENNIALS

Variety	Season	Color & Height	Comments
Achillea 'Coronation Gold' (Yarrow)	Late Spring through Summer	Yellow 3 ft.	- Excellent as a dried flower - Very hardy - Flowers last over two weeks - Full sun
Alyssum 'Basket of Gold'	Spring	Yellow 12-15 inches	- Good for borders - Cascades over walls - Self seeds - Sun
Aquilegia (Columbine)	Spring	Yellow, white, lavender, pink, bicolor. 12-18 inches	- Delicate flower - Susceptible to leaf miner - Cut off seed pods to extend plant's life - Partial shade to sun
Arabis (Candytuft)	Spring	White 10 inches	- Excellent border plant - Shear back for second flowering - Full sun
Asclepsis (Butterfly weed)	Summer	Bright orange 24 inches	- Attracts butterflies - Seed pods similar to milkweed - Aphids may be a problem - Full sun
Asters	Fall	Purple, pink, and white 18-24 inches	- Blooms up to frost - Excellent cut flower - Some varieties may need staking - Full sun
Astilbe	Spring and early Summer	Pink, red and white	- "Feathery" flowers - Excellent as a dried flower - Semi-shade
Baptisia	Spring	Blue 30 inches	- Spiked flower - Leaves are similar to the pea plant - Semi-shade to full sun
Centaurea montana	Spring and early Summer	Blue 18-24 inches	- Flowers are similar to bachelor buttons - Outside leaves may be cut back after first flowering new plant will form in center

PERENNIALS

Variety	Season	Color & Height	Comments
Chrysanthemum superba (Shasta Daisy)	Late Summer into Fall	White 24 inches	- Large white daisy flowers - Good cut flower - Blooms second year from seed - Full sun
Chrysanthemum "Pot mums"	Fall	White, yellow, rust, pink, purple and burgundy 2-3 feet	- These are borderline plants for me, they must be mulched in winter and I still lose some. - Full sun
Coreopsis	Summer	Yellow 18 inches	- Small daisy-like flowers - Full sun
Dicentra (Bleeding heart)	Spring	Pink, white 30 inches	- Excellent Spring flower - Makes a lovely combination with Spring bulbs and perennials - Shade or semi-shade
Digitalis (Foxglove)	Summer	pink, yellow, lavender and white 24-36 inches	- Biennial, self seeds, blooms second year after planting - Tall showy flowers - Full sun to semi-shade
Geranium Cranesbill (Hardy)	Spring into Summer	pink and lavender 12-15 inches	- Low growing, spreads quickly - A true geranium, not the pelargonium variety grown in the summer - Sun
Gypsophilia (Baby's breath)	Summer	White or pink 3-4 feet	- Delicate airy flowers - Needs staking - Mulch in winter - Sun or semi-shade
Hemerocallis (Daylily)	Summer	Yellow and shades of orange 3 feet	- Very hardy - May be divided every three years - Full sun to semi-shade
Heuchera (Coral bells)	Spring	Pink and red	- Delicate flowers on tall stalks that rise from a mound of scalloped foliage - Semi-shade

PERENNIALS

Variety	Season	Color & Height	Comments
Hosta	Spring through Fall	Green or green and white foliage lavender flowers	- Excellent shade plant - Used for foliage rather than flowers - Deer may be a problem, they love this plant
Iris	Spring	White, yellow, purple, and bicolor 3 feet	- Very showy flowers - Bearded iris susceptible to iris borer - Siberian iris smaller - Full sun
Lamium (Dead nettle)	Spring through Fall	Pink or white flowers silver and green foliage 6-12 inches	- Flowers all season - Very hardy, mine sometimes stays green all winter - Excellent ground cover - Semi-shade or sun
Limonium (Sea lavender)	Summer	White or lavender 18-24 inches	- Flowers rise on long stalks from a center of leathery leaves - Excellent dried flower - Full sun
Lupine	Spring	Purple, white and pink 30 inches	- Spike flowers - Does better in cooler climates, some gardeners in the area grow it successfully
Mertensia (Virginia bluebells)	Spring	Blue 12-18 inches	- Lovely spring flower - Mark location when plant dies back to avoid disturbing - Shade or semi-shade
Monarda (Beebalm)	Summer	Red, pink, lavender and white	- Attracts bees and hummingbirds - Use in back of the border - Susceptible to mildew - Full sun
Oenothera (Evening Primrose)	Spring	Yellow	- Flower resembles large buttercup - Excellent for shade or semi-shade - Spreads quickly
Papaver (Poppy)	Spring	Orange, pink red 18-24 inches	- May choke out more desireable plants - Foliage dies back in July - Very showy flowers - Sun

PERENNIALS

Variety	Season	Color & Height	Comments
Paeonia (Peony)	Spring	Red, pink, white 2-4 feet	- Spectacular blossoms, often very fragrant - Shrubby plant, does not like to be moved after it is established
Phlox	Summer	White, pink burgundy, bicolored 3-4 feet	- Needs staking - Very showy flowers - Susceptible to mildew, give good air circulation - Sun to semi-shade
Platycodon (Balloon flower)	Summer	White, pink, blue 20 inches	- Plant emerges very late in Spring, be careful not to disturb - Needs staking - Semi-shade
Pulmonaria (Lungwort)	Spring	Pink flowers spotted foliage	- Foliage adds color after flowers die - Shade or semi-shade - Wilts in hot weather, needs moist soil
Rudbeckia (Black-eyed Susan)	Summer	Yellow 24-30 inches	- Good cut flower - Sun
Sedum 'Autumn Gold'	Fall	Red 18-24 inches	- Flower goes from light green to deep red in the Fall - Full sun
Veronica	Spring into Summer	Blue 18 inches	- Spiked flowers - Attracts bees and butterflies - Full sun
Violets	Spring	Blue, white, variegated	- Excellent ground cover for shade spreads quickly - Shade or semi-shade - Good Spring color

5

Let's Grow Herbs

By Sandy Greig

The enchantment of the herb garden lies in the perfect union of usefulness and beauty. The plants specific to the catagory "herbs" delight our senses with mystical fragrances, exotic tastes, brillant colors, subtle textures and provide suitable companionship for vegetables, butterflies and hummingbirds, and the gentlest spirit that resides in us all.

No matter what your favorite hobby, you may eventually become an herb ethusiast. If you like to raise sheep or spin wool, by and by you will be tempted to dye your own yarns. If perfumery is your interest, herbs have wonderful fragrances to add to your flowers. Herbs hold the secrets to medical self-help. And one sure way not to become bored with your own cooking is to use herbs to full advantage.

You don't need a large plot of land to encourage your interest. Herbs can be a useful addition to the vegetable garden as natural pest repellents and are suitable as terrace plants or window garden greens when planted in pots. There is a certain charm about the perfectly designed formal herb garden - how nice to project our inner balance - but the wild and free form that suits most herbs allows a presentation of abandon - how rugged and enduring these perennials can be!

GROWING HERBS

The Plant Characteristics Chart (5-1) describes the best methods of propagation for the most common herbs. Delightfully, once most perennials herbs are established in the garden, they can be easily separated into more plants from year to year. Annuals have a one season lifespan but are sometimes prone to self-seeding, whereby nature replenishes herself.

In designing an herb garden, give attention to the height and nature of the individual plants. The subtle shades of green to gray to silver should also be considered to add texture and color balance to the scheme. Place tall plants at the back, shorter ones to the front of the border to create a harmonious appearance and also to facilitate harvest.

As a plant family, herbs are the least demanding for regular watering and fertilizing. Many herbs originated in the Mediterranean climate where the growing conditions of dry, rocky soil and minimum moisture insured that these plants had to be tough to survive. The fragrance and flavor of herbs comes from the high concentration of volatile oil within the leaf. As a general rule, the concentration of oil is greatest just as the flowers begin to form on the stem. Nature is asserting herself toward the rejuvenation of the species by developing seed, and musters up the greatest energy within the plant. The Harvest and Storage Guide (5-2) will be helpful to find the exceptions to this rule. It also notes which plant parts are useful and the best methods of storage.

The day before harvest, if possible, spray the plants with water to remove dust. Allow the plants to dry completely of dew before cutting. Any water will cause dark discoloration during the drying process. Herbs that are to be air dried should be tied with string in bunches no larger than what can be encircled with the thumb and index finger. Larger bunches might cause mold to grow at the tied part. The bunches should be hung with stem ends up in a warm, dry place with adequate ventilation out of direct sunlight. A quick drying time will insure the strongest flavor and fragrance and also retain the best color for visual enjoyment. Individual leaves can be set on screens and dried in the same manner. Drying time varies from species to species and is also dependent on the weather, but most herbs dry within 10 days. Depending on your proximity to the Hudson River where humidity factors are a major consideration, thick, fleshy leaves may take more time to dry and as a result, may turn brown in the drying process. Basil is one that can prove difficult. For fast drying, it is advisable to dry the herb leaves on a cookie sheet in a warm oven. The lowest possible setting is usually sufficient. The leaves will dry in about two hours.

Once the leaves seem dry (they should be crisp and crumble easily), whether from the oven or tied in bunches, they are best kept in glass storage jars or tins to prevent moisture reabsorption and loss of flavor from volatile oil evaporation. Leaves can be stripped from the stems to save space but an attempt should be made to keep the leaves as whole as possible. Volatile oil escapes at any fracture. The tins should be kept away from direct sun to prevent bleaching and away from heat. After the first 24 hours in storage, check the jars for any signs of moisture that will be released if the herbs are not thoroughly dry. If there is moisture visible in the jars, it is necessary to remove the leaves and place them on screens or cookie sheets for a day or two more. Any retained moisture will cause mold to grow and render your harvest unusable.

For some culinary and medicinal herbs, freezing is a quick and easy way to retain flavor as well as perfect color. Herbs can be harvested from the garden, wrapped in foil or sealed in plastic, have great advantage with this method as they can be taken from the freezer, a portion chopped from the frozen block and the rest re-- turned to the freezer immediately for use the next time.

The flavor, fragrance and medicinal application of various herbs can also be stored in vinegars, oils, and tisanes. Colors for herbal dye baths can be made and frozen for future use.

USING YOUR HARVEST

Herb crafting becomes an adventure in creativity. Cooking with herbs is the most obvious solution for use. But simply speaking, herbs can improve the quality of your life. Nothing is so satisfying as to start with a tiny, little seed and in the end, beautify your home, tickle your senses or ease someone else's overtired spirit with the harvest of your hands, heart and mind. The Chart for Common Uses (5-3) describes generally the broadest applications of the common herbs listed.

Herbal teas can be used for social or medicinal purposes. Social teas are usually infused; the herbs are covered with boiling water and allowed to steep 3-5 minutes. Longer steeping will release tannin, a bitter oil, and will make the tea acrid. Medicinal teas, on the other hand, sometimes require these tannins to become effective, and therefore are decocted by boiling the herb in water for a specific length of time. Fresh herbs for a social tea should be measured 1 tablespoon per cup. Dried herbs are more concentrated, so 1 teaspoon per cup is recommended.

Fresh or preserved herbs can be added to food as seasoning. Dried herbs are 3 times as strong as fresh and should be used with discretion. Experience is the best teacher. The addition of herbs in cooking can add flavors that enhance foods and provide the option to eliminate salt. This is especially useful to people on restricted diets. Bits of dried herb leaves can be combined to make herb blends.

Cosmetic herbs can be combined to add relaxation to the bath (lavender, mints and comphrey), tintilation to the footbath (pine needles, calendula and lavender for fragrance), and stimulation to the facial sauna (mints, lemon herbs and camomile). Using herbs to make creams, salves, shampoos and hair rinses shows how special you are to yourself.

Potpourri is a combination of herb leaves and flower petals, fragrance and fixative used to perfume rooms, closets or bureau drawers. Its purpose is to smell nice and to add fragrance to that-which is around it. Potpourris can be more purposeful when herbs are combined to act as a moth repellent, odor eating sneaker stuffer and sick room refresher.

Herbs can be dried to use later for flower arrangements, herb wreaths and tussie-mussies. Herb wreaths can be strictly for decoration or can be designed in theme, i.e. culinary wreaths of cooking herbs, moth repellent herbs to hang inside a closet or historical wreaths made of ancient or colonial herbs. In the language of flowers, all herbs have symbolic meanings. Herbs can be used in combination to fashion a message in the form of a bouquet. These are called tussie-mussies. These make a welcome gift for a friend as each herb included denotes sentiment.

TIPS FROM A DUTCHESS COUNTY GARDENER

There are many very good books on all facets of herb growing readily available on the market. In general, the advice contained is universal. If this chapter inspires further knowledge, indulge yourself. But remember that our region is unique, and you may come across some information that is right for southern California, but wrong for us. Briefly, listed below are some hints to make local growing more satisfying.

- **Artemesia** — Replant every two years to get the broadest branching.

- **Basil** — Do not overlook the many variants on this species. Lemon (broiled on chicken or fish) and cinnamon (added to fresh flower arrangements for fragrance) are especially delicious. Harvest basil before frost as it is very tender and the first to die back in the fall.

- **Borage** — Learn to recognize the leaves. This is a generous self-seeder and one planting will last a lifetime if you know not to pull the new seedlings out as weeds in the spring.

- **Catnip** — Go for the *Mussini* variety. The inflorescence is beyond compare.

- **Chamomile** — A natural self-seeder. Useful for field or steep rise plantings.

- **Dill** — Another self-seeder. Plant in a place where it can grow from year to year. It will establish a never ending supply within a few years.

- **Garlic** — The most flavorful varieties must be started to encourage a fall flowering.

- **Hyssop** — Prune the plant following the first flowering to encourage a fall flowering.

- **Lavender** — *Vera*, *Augustifolia* and *Munstead*, prove to be the most winter hardy.

- **Parsley** — Plan to replant every year.

- **Rosemary** — Plant specimens in clay pots and sink them in the garden. Water well the first few weeks. These are not winter hardy and should be lifted, pot and all, in the fall and brought indoors in winter. This is a treat as it flowers at Christmas time.

- **Sage** — The perennial blue flowering variety is the most common. But try *clary* sage for the beautiful flowers (biennial) and also *pineapple* sage for variety.

- **Thyme** — Be aware of self-seeders in the spring. They are abundant.

PREPARING YOUR GARDEN FOR WINTER

Certainly after your first season you will be committed to enjoying the herb garden in years to come. Some precautions for winter must be exercised to ensure repeated pleasures.

A final harvest can be taken from the plants about 3 weeks before the first anticipated frost. This allows the plants to grow on a bit before cold weather when growth stops. New growth provides insulation for the plants through the winter. Annuals can be pulled from the garden and the ground gently cultivated to help nature with the self-seeding. Perennials that require mulching should be dressed with evergreen boughs, not leaves. Evergreens provide air circulation which is necessary so the plants do not smother. Leaves as mulch cause base rotting which will kill the plants. Since perennial herbs are really quite hardy, mulch may be pulled off in the early spring without fear of damage.

An herb garden, perhaps more than any other planting, offers a continuum not totally unlike life itself. Over time it evolves to its greatest potential by your care, interest and awareness and repays your efforts with a sight of beauty unfolding, the enrichment of life, and joy in being partners with nature.

5-1 PLANT CHARACTERISTICS

HERB	LIFESPAN*	PROPAGATION	HEIGHT AND NATURE
ARTEMESIAS	P	Division	2' upright
BASIL	A	Seed	2-3' upright
BORAGE	A	Seed, self seeds	12" rosette
BURNET	P	Seed	18" upright
CALENDULA	A	Seed, self seeds	18" upright
CATNIP	P	Seed/Division	18" bushy
CHAMOMILE	A&P	Seed/Self sows	12-30" spreading
CHIVES	P	Seed/Division	12" clumps
DILL	A	Seed, self seeds	2-3' willowy
HOREHOUND	P	Seed/Cuttings	2' trailing
HYSSOP	P	Seed, self seeds	18" hedge
LAVENDER	P,tender	Seed/Cuttings	1-2' bushy
LEMON BALM	P	Seed/Cuttings	to 2½' spreading
MARJORAM	P	Seed/Cuttings	to 2' spreading
MINTS	P	Root division	2-3' spreading
NASTURTIUM	A	Seed	18" trailing
OREGANO	P	Seed/Division	to 2½' spreading
PARSLEY	B	Seed	18" rosette
ROSEMARY	P,tender	Seed/Cutting	to 6' upright
RUE	P	Seed	2½" upright
SAGE	P	Seed/Division	2' bushy
SAVORY	A&P	Seed/Division	18" trailing
SCENTED GERANIUMS	Potted	Cutting	to 3'
TANSY	P	Seed, self seeds	4' bushy
TARRAGON	P	Cutting	18" trailing
THYME	P	Seed, self sows	12" spreading
YARROW	P	Division	2½' bush

* Annual, Perennial or Biennial

5-2 HARVEST AND STORAGE GUIDE

	As needed	Pre-flower	In flower	Leaf	Seed	Flower	Dry	Freeze	Vinegar
	HARVEST			PARTS			STORE		
Artemesia		X		X			X		
Basil	X	X		X			X	X	X
Borage	X			X	X	X			
Calendula	X		X			X	X		
Catnip	X	X		X			X		
Chamomile			X			X	X		
Chives	X		X	X		X		X	X
Dill	X			X	X	X	X	X	X
Horehound		X		X			X		
Hyssop		X		X			X		
Lavender	X		X	X		X	X		
Lemon Balm	X			X			X		
Marjoram	X	X		X			X		X
Nasturtium	X		X	X		X			
Oregano	X	X		X			X		X
Parsley	X			X				X	
Mints	X			X			X		
Rosemary	X			X			X		X
Sage	X			X			X		
Savory		X		X			X		
Tansy	X		X	X		X	X		
Tarragon	X			X			X		X
Thyme	X			X			X		X
Yarrow	X		X	X		X	X		

5-3 Herb Growers Chart for Common Uses

	TEA	SEASONING	MEDICINAL	COSMETIC	POTPOURRI	ARRANGEMENTS
Artemesia			X			X
Basil		X			X	
Borage	X			X		
Calendula		X	X		X	X
Catnip	X		X		X	
Chamomile	X		X	X	X	
Chive		X				X
Dill		X				X
Horehound	X		X			
Hyssop	X		X			
Lavender				X	X	X
Lemon Balm	X	X		X	X	
Marjoram		X			X	
Mints	X	X	X	X		
Nasturtium		X				X
Oregano		X				
Parsley		X	X			
Rosemary	X	X	X	X	X	
Sage	X	X	X		X	
Savory		X				X
Tansy			X	X		X
Tarragon		X				
Thyme		X	X		X	
Yarrow	X		X		X	X

Tussie-Mussie

In the language of flowers, all herbs have symbolic meanings. A tussie-mussie is a small bouquet made of herbs and flowers selected to make a statement by their symbolism. This can be made of fresh or dried material. If fresh, it can be dried as a keepsake. The prettier ones are set in lace doilies and the stems are tied with ribbons. But any way you do it, it's easy to "say it with flowers". Below is a list of the more common herbs and their meanings.

Basil	Love or hate
Bay	Victory or reward
Borage	Courage
Burnet	A merry heart
Calendula	Grief
Caraway	Retention
Chamomile	Patience
Fennel	Praise
Horehound	Health
Lavender	Acknowledgement
Lemon Balm	Sociability, Sympathy
Lemon Verbena	Delicacy of feelings
Mints	Virtue, Wisdom
Rosemary	Rememberance
Rue	Disdain
Sage	Esteem, Long life
Marjoram	Happiness
Tansy	Hostility
Thyme	Activity, Bravery
Wormwood	Absence, Displeasure
Yarrow	To sooth a headache

6

Let's Grow Vegetables

By Bob Piggott

First, The GOOD news! You don't have to be an extensive land owner to be a successful vegetable grower. In fact, on many occasions the champion vegetable entries at the Dutchess County Fair were from "backyard" gardeners.

The bad news is, that the more involved you get, the more you discover that you don't know. However, when it comes to dinnertime you'll certainly agree that the pluses outweigh the minuses!

As reasonably active gardeners for many years, we have come to feel that a moderate degree of success in vegetable growing can be achieved by giving careful thought and planning to four considerations.

- First - What to plant (including varieties)
- Second - Where to plant
- Third - When to plant
- Fourth - When to harvest
- There are, of course, other "minor" matters to consider such as proper moisture, weed control, disease control and pest control, but as they are being considered in other sections of this book, we'll assume that you'll do a good job in diligently researching the most acceptable practices in all these matters.

START WITH SEED

It's often been said, that perhaps the first sign of spring is the arrival (usually in January) of the annual seed catalog, complete with colored pictures of fruits, vegetables and flowers in their full glorious summer bloom. While you should keep in mind that your results probably won't be as photogenic as the items depicted, the catalog is probably a good place to start.

Most veteran gardeners will know that there are literally dozens of seed catalogs available, but the novice might be interested in knowing how to obtain some of the more common ones. Please consider these suggestions as only a means for getting started and for comparison.

Harris Moran Seed Company
3670 Buffalo Road
Rochester, New York 14624

W. Atlee Burpee Seed Company
Warminster, Pa. 18974

Asgrow Seed Company
Kalamazoo, Michigan 49001

Gurney Seed & Nursery Co.
Yankton, S. Dakota 57078

Most of these catalogs do a good job of describing the many obtainable vegetable varieties as well as keeping you up to date on new ones constantly being developed. Notes are also generally included as to best geographical locations and disease tolerances for most of your selections.

In an effort to confuse you readers, I would comment at this point, that varieties we grow today will probably change tomorrow — and probably weren't available yesterday.

Old Timers remember names like *Bonny Best*, *Rutgers*, *Marglobe*, *Country Gentleman* and *Golden Bantam* as some of the most popular kinds of tomatoes and sweet corn. Today, you'd have to search to find a source for the few of these that may still be available. Why? Because tastes change, newer varieties are hardier, perhaps larger and possibly more attractive. And so it goes — what we'll recommend in this chapter will probably change in the next decade as a whole new generation of gardeners prepares to face the challenge.

GETTING STARTED

As you make the first big decision, "what to grow", try to keep in mind a few essentials. Some vegetables take much more room than others and some would be better off isolated from the rest of the garden.

The amount of space available for your garden becomes a very important factor. My best suggestion, if your plot is limited in size, would be to pass over items such as sweet corn, pumpkins and spreading varieties of squash. While we understand that corn is a summer favorite, many home gardeners don't realize that is takes at least four rows - planted two to three feet apart to get proper pollination - unless you're ready to spend the time to help Mother Nature by hand. For the amount of pumpkins and winter squash most families use - your garden space would be better devoted to the many vegetables either more compact or that can be trained to climb. Therefore, here's what we would suggest to get the most out of your small, backyard garden.

Assuming that you don't want (or have the facilities) to grow seedlings indoors - we'd recommend tilling your soil as soon as frost leaves in the spring. If possible, locate your garden in a well drained, sunlit area. Should organic fertilizer be available, spread it before turning the ground. Commercial fertilizers can also be incorporated at planting time or as a side dressing later. In either case, remember that they tend to be quite powerful and can burn as well as nurture your plants.

LET'S GROW

By the first week in April, you should be ready to consider planting the following: Peas, or if you like them - Sugar Peas, are an early tradition. For the conventional kind, we've had very good luck with *Greater Progress* - a Harris variety. Be sure to put them 3-4 inches deep in a well fertilized section of your garden. Remember, that peas can climb - so consider a low wire or string fence later on. At this time you can also plant some lettuce, radishes and if conditions are right and space permits you can put in spinach, collards, swiss chard or kale to be followed by seedlings of cabbage, brussel sprouts, cauliflower and broccoli. For the broccoli, we favor *Green Comet* and note that *Prince Marvel* is replacing the traditional *Jade Cross* sprouts. *Bravo* is a good new hybrid cabbage and *Snowball 123* is a promising new cauliflower variety.

6-1 Brussels Sprouts,
for something different.

6-2 Chantenay carrots are stubby
for our soil.

We don't recommend any specific lettuce or radish variety as there are numerous good ones available. However, you would probably be happier with leaf lettuce than attempting the "iceberg" or heading varieties - and a trick we learned long ago is to sow (sparingly) your carrot seeds with your radishes - since they take considerably longer to germinate and could get lost to weeds if planted later in the season. Therefore - if you follow this procedure, be sure to pull all the radishes as early as possible to give the carrots growing room. By the way, we lean toward a *Nantes* or *Chantenay* variety carrot.

Some folks like home grown onions, and since they don't take much space and can be pulled early, consider them for your April planting. Sets can be obtained from many seed companies or most local farm centers. For best results keep them apart about 6" and don't be afraid to fertilize once they're established. Many growers consider Bone Meal an excellent nutrient for onion type crops. If you're a leek and/or celery buff, remember that they are generally grown from seed and if you can't start some indoors, April is none too early. The same, by the way, goes for parsley.

While thinking of parsley (and *Banquet* is excellent if you like the curled type), lot's of folks enjoy it as a garnish year-round by sowing seeds in a large flower pot in mid-summer and bringing it inside in October. You also get the side benefits of an attractive plant with a nice, fresh garden odor.

By the first week in May, even the faint hearted gardeners can begin to think seriously about getting started. For them, the items already mentioned should be planted pronto! However, for you veterans who by now are observing many of your early plantings already growing, it's time to think of your main summer crops. Next to sweet corn, the big summer winner is usually tomatoes.

Our advice here may come as a shock if you're of the "Memorial Day" planting advocates - but **especially** for the backyard gardener, if you want early tomatoes (by July 4th) get them in now! A few plants should cause no problems with covering, since even a large grocery bag will do - and in the unlikely event that you do catch a late frost, the worst that can happen is that you'll have to plant again. Incidentally, telling this "secret" is like killing the goose that lays the golden egg, because one of the stocks-in-trade at our farm market is selling early tomatoes to the end-of-May planters at a good price!

As with most vegetables, tomato varieties change almost yearly. At this time, we are using, and would recommend *Jet Star* or *Pik Red* for your early plants to be followed by either *Supersonic* or *Beefmaster* for later enjoyment.

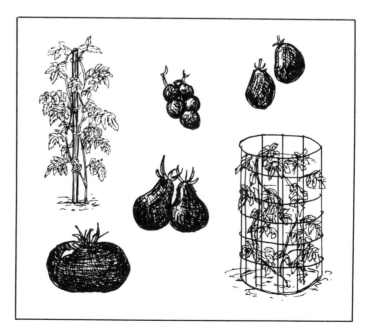

6-3 Tomatoes come in many shapes and sizes. Upper left, staked tomato plant. Lower right, tomato cage.

GROWING TIPS

Again, depending on your space, we would suggest the following growing tips. Purchase a roll of black plastic mulch from your local farm center and after laying it carefully, plant thru holes cut every two or three feet apart. Incidentally, while speaking of plastic mulch - we recommend it highly for use whenever and wherever possible. You will get better yields, keep your vegetables cleaner and your ground will stay moist much longer under dry conditions. It also makes for a lot less weeding! If more than one row is desired, keep them at least three feet wide also. If space is limited, take advantage of the metal "cages" now available - or stake and tie your plants. Remember, tomatoes like lots of sunshine and while they need considerable watering, soil that is constantly wet can be devastating. While information concerning insects and disease will be covered elsewhere, we do suggest a regular spraying - starting when blossoms appear - with both a good fungicide and an effective pesticide. Many are available on the market and since spraying in general is a very touchy subject, we feel that each individual must act according to his own dictates.

6-4 Vegetable plants growing on plastic mulch.

By the second week of May, most of your vegetables grown from seed can be started with almost no chance of frost damage. For most folks, these would include both cucumbers and beans.

However, for best results, we recommend planting them in separate parts of your garden. The reason - cucumbers can be a bit of a renegade, particularly if they contract Downy Mildew, Powdery Mildew or Cucumber Mosaic. It's been our experience (learned years ago- the hard way) that if these diseases strike - they'll very likely transfer to your beans, melons and other crops. The same can be said incidentally, for the family lilac bush - it too, while showing no apparant signs of disease, can be a prolific carrier of plant mosaic and should be better kept away from your vegetable garden.

OF CUKES AND BEANS

Back to cucumbers. Once again, you'll find dozens of varieties available - both Hybrid and Open Pollinated. As a rule, your hybrids are more expensive - particularly if you prefer the "burpless" variety. However, while most of these are excellent, we have had a good degree of success with *Pacer* for the early crop, followed by an old standard - *Marketmore* for later eating. For those of you with very limited space, most local greenhouse operators can provide you with several trellis or climbing types, which, while not cheap, are interesting to grow and can make a good conversation piece.

Meanwhile, back in the bean patch...if you're like us and really enjoy beans, this is a vegetable you should plant every 10 days or so to keep a continuous supply available right into the fall. Our favorites at the present time are *Provider* for green beans and *Sungold* for the yellow wax type. If we were inclined to use the pole variety, no doubt we would be using the old standby, *Kentucky Wonder*. For the small garden, pole beans could well be your best bet - both for the added space left over and because your beans will be nearly all off the ground, which could prevent some rotting problems in wet weather.

While speaking of beans - we are very partial to lima beans -and an old country favorite when they're combined with sweet corn - succotash. Our longtime favorite lima is the *Fordhook 242* variety - which can be disease prone when conditions are too wet, but in a good growing season, produces an abundance of uniform, delicious beans. We have found mid-May the best time to plant these - and a second planting in early June could add fresh treats later on.

BOB PIGGOT'S VEGETABLE VARIETY RECOMMENDATIONS:

Peas:	*Greater Progress*
Broccoli:	*Green Comet*
Brussel sprouts:	*Prince Marvel*
Cabbage:	*Bravo*
Cauliflower:	*Snowball 123*
Carrot:	*Nates*
	Chantenay
Parsley:	*Banquet*
Tomatoes:	*Jet Star*
	Pik Red
	Supersonic
	Beefmaster
Cucumber:	*Pacer*
	Marketmore
Green beans:	*Provider*
Yellow beans:	*Sungold*
Pole beans:	*Kentucky Wonder*
Lima beans:	*Fordhook 242*
Beets:	*Crosby Green Top*
	Warrior
Peppers:	*Ace*
	Lady Belle
Eggplant:	*Black Magic*
Potatoes:	*Superior*
	Katahdins
	Norlands
Muskmelon:	*Gold Star*
	Superstar
Squash:	*Zucchini Elite*
	Seneca Prolific
	Table King
	Butter (Early Butternut Hybrid)
	Buttercup (Burgess Strain)
Pumpkin:	*Jackpot*

MORE FAVORITES

Another standard vegetable that's good for you and offers double possibilities is the lowly beet. Actually, they're one of the easier ones to grow and as they are thinned - the greens make an excellent substitute for spinach, with perhaps an even better flavor. Here again, two crops are possible, with the earlier one producing perhaps the nicer greens. We lean toward *Crosby Green Top* , while a friend has had good luck with *Warrior*. Remember, beets taste best while still relatively small and are a good source of iron.

According to recent studies, another "good for you" vegetable is the often neglected Brussel Sprouts. Most folks don't put them high on a priority list, but if properly cooked, they can be tasty as well as nutritious. If you start them from seed, sow early, as mentioned before - but it might be easier obtaining a few plants from you favorite garden center. Since sprouts take quite a while before fully maturing, you may tend to forget about them - but, as with most vegetables, we recommend a regular spraying with a good insecticide. Once you start picking, with any kind of luck, you can continue right up until the first snowfall.

We feel that no garden would be complete without some peppers and eggplant. These can both be planted (from nursery stock) by the middle of May. Both of these common vegetables have caused us problems in the past, but our best advice would be to transplant very carefully and particularly with the eggplant, spray weekly for insect control. They are susceptible to both flea beetles and the Colorado Potato Beetle. Regarding variety, we have had good luck with both *Ace* and *Lady Bell* peppers and *Black Magic* eggplant. The pepper varieties mentioned tend to germinate consistently and offer a reliable yield year after year.

THE BASIC POTATO

Speaking of the Colorado Potato Beetle, it occurs to us that many of you may want to devote some space to perhaps the most basic vegetable, potatoes. If this is the case, remember first that potatoes like a slightly acid soil and that they seem more prone every year to beetle infestation. As with most vegetables, there are a wealth of varieties to choose from and the ultimate decision must be yours. Most growers favor *Superior,* for the early digging and we feel that *Katahdins* offer the best results for later harvest. Some gardeners like the early red variety - *Norlands*, and we agree that they offer a fine alternative. Even though potatoes are mentioned at this point in the chapter, it is most desirable to get them in early-certainly by April 15th. With any kind of luck, they should be ready for digging by mid-July and will continue to develop for the remainder of the summer.

There is considerable room for argument over how to plant potatoes (some even advocate placing them on top of the ground and covering liberally with hay), but our best advice is to set them apart and cover evenly. Then, as they mature, we think that hilling will make for bigger and better yields.

Another favorite for many people are any of the varieties of home grown melons. We are particularly partial to cantaloupe (or muskmelons), while others enjoy the larger crenshaws or the green or orange honeydews. Some folks have expressed a preference for the less heralded, but equally tasty casabas and persian melons. Whatever your choice, melons will make a very tasty addition to your garden and require only good sunlight and the same care you give to your other vine type plants. We are partial to Harris-Moran *Gold Star* or *Superstar* muskmelons, but there are many interesting types to choose from - so don't be afraid to experiment.

Planting wise - we generally sow seeds (about 5 to a hill) in the latter part of May. Depending on the variety, this should assure a good crop sometime before Labor Day. It should be noted that some varieties are more susceptible to blight, fusarium wilt or mildew than others - so a regular spraying with a good fungicide is recommended. It's also a good idea to keep melons away from any area where standing water might occur (which is true for nearly all vegetables) and when your fruit begins to show some size, placing a piece of plastic, paper of other light cover under as many specimens as possible should help insure excellent mature melons. Incidentally, we think that - as mentioned before - your melons will do much better, if kept away from your cucumbers.

SQUASH AND MORE SQUASH

We earlier mentioned that some vine-type crops might take up too much garden space, but this should not include the ever popular zucchini and the traditional yellow summer squash. Both of these versatile vegetables are relatively easy to grow - and do exceedingly well if grown over black plastic. For years, we have grown *Zucchini Elite* and *Seneca Prolific* for the yellow variety. As with most crops, better results will occur if you spray regularly with both an insecticide and fungicide. Our current preference for these controls are Sevin and Manzate, which can be effectively mixed in powder form in a small back-pack sprayer (follow label directions).

One of the finest features of both yellow and zucchini type squash is that, if picked regularly (on an every second day basis) they will produce a bountiful crop for the better part of the summer. A late planting (in early July) should insure a continuation of these popular vegetables until frost.

While on the subject of picking - it should be noted that if you continue to pick the second growth broccoli spears every second or third day, they too will continue to produce until fall. This is a feature to consider when deciding what to include in your garden.

Even though we previously stated (and rightly so), that certain vegetables would require too much space for serious consideration in a small, backyard garden - the thought occurs that perhaps some of you will have more room and do really enjoy growing and eating winter squash. With this in mind, perhaps the first thing to consider would be whether your favorite is available in some of the newer bush or semi-bush varieties. Certain types of acorn, such as *Table King*, Butternut (*Early Butternut Hybrid*), and Buttercup (*Burgess Strain*) are available in this compact form. Incidentally, the same is true for the recently developed *Jackpot* pumpkin.

Our favorite eating squash for the winter season is Buttercup, which is dark green, round, with a silverish tip showing through on the blossom end. Planting direction - which hold true for most members of the squash family simply are to sow seed in hills (about three per hill) and space them about four feet apart. If your squash is the spreading vine type, put them on the edge of your garden and train the vines toward the outside. This could give you less lawn to mow - an extra benefit! Planting can be done nearly anytime from mid-May through early July. For you early planters, picking will commence before Labor Day. Once again, we suggest spraying weekly with both insecticide and a fungicide.

HAPPY GARDENING

So much for "what to plant". If you successfully wade through all the items mentioned and get to enjoy some of each - give yourself a blue ribbon for being a first prize gardener!

It should be noted that most vegetables are best if picked on the young side (we love fingerling carrots) and some, like tomatoes and melons will continue to ripen after picking.

Many vegetables can be planted periodically for staggered crops or late crops. Notable among these are radishes, lettuce, beets, cabbage, broccoli and beans. We consider early August none too late for the ones mentioned.

Finally - as the gardening "bug" gets you, don't be afraid to experiment and try some of the less well known items such as Okra and Kolrabi. Also, for the gourmet gardeners, a full assortment of your favorite herbs are available.

We'd like to remind the reader that the one truism we've learned over the years is, that the more you grow, the more you discover that you don't know. However - the key word is, persevere! Happy gardening.

7

Let's Grow Berries and Grapes

By Joe Indelicato

STRAWBERRIES

Strawberries are one of the easiest and most rewarding fruits I have ever grown. And they will grow in just about any location that gets full sun—a patch, a border or scattered hills among your other flowers or vegetables. One of the nicest things about having your own strawberry patch is opening a jar of freezer jam in mid-winter. I have never tasted a cooked strawberry jam that captured the fresh summer flavor of the berries prepared this way. We always made enough jam for the year and enjoyed fresh berries during the season—all this from a patch 10' by 20'. My choice was a June-bearing berry passed along to me by a neighbor (Unfortunately, I never knew what variety this wonderful producer was). If you are not interested in the volume needed for jams and jellies, but would prefer to be able to pick over an extended period during both early summer and late summer, then your choice would be an ever-bearing variety.

You can purchase your plants through one of the many catalogs sent to your home or through a local nursery or farm supply store. These usually come in bunches of 25 (rather dried-up) plants with planting instructions included. Nurseries should also have available during the planting season potted plants—these cost more but the success rate is much better. What-ever source you use should have recommended varieties of both June-bearing and everbearing berries for this area. I have checked with some local growers and the following have been successful producers for them:

> *Early Glow* — June bearing (early season)
> *Catskill* — June bearing (mid-season)
> *Sparkle* — June bearing (late-season)
> *Ozark Beauty* — everbearing

Once you have decided what your needs are and the type of berry you will grow, the planting and maintenance of your patch is quite easy. Hopefully you will spend more time bending over to pick than to maintain this delicious fruit.

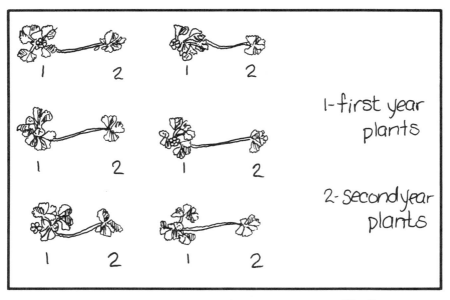

7-1 Strawberry bed, spacing for maximum space utilization.

You can set plants out as soon as the ground can be worked in the spring. This is usually late March or early April in the Hudson Valley. If you plan on a patch, plant your rows 18 to 24 inches apart. Keep in mind that once your patch is established, you will be shifting rows every year or two—rooting runners in the clear space between rows and then removing the old plants. Diagram (7-1) illustrates the system I have used successfully for many years. With more space available, I would use a propagation system such as that shown in diagram (7-2). Since maximum production is usually on plants that are two years old, this system seems to me the ideal. The spacing is, in my opinion, one of the most important factors in abundant production. I remember my first efforts being rewarded with a large, lush green patch; I was sure a huge crop was underway. Without enough sun and air circulation around each plant, however, my reward was a few small, mildewed berries. Set plants into holes large enough to accommodate roots. They should be set just deep enough to cover roots but leave crown of plant exposed. Once the plants begin to develop new leaves you can fertilize them. Manure is my preference as I have plenty available, but commercial fertilizer should work just as well. A mulch will prevent weeds and retain moisture in the roots; it will also protect the berries from ground moisture while they are ripening. The best mulch I have found is, not suprisingly, straw. It allows drainage, deters weed growth, and, unlike mulch hay, will not sprout. During the first year, the new plants will produce a few blossoms. Pinch these off to encourage plant growth, and each year thereafter your patch will produce for you.

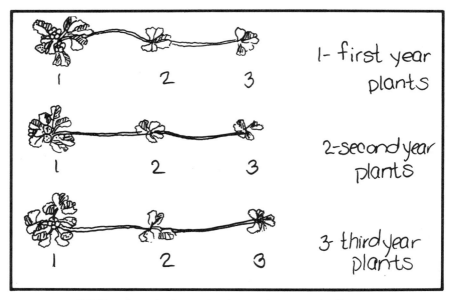

7-2 Strawberry bed, spacing for maximum production.

Though strawberries are easy to grow, there are a few problems that might affect the quantity and quality of your harvest. Pests I have dealt with are birds and squirrels. They are as fond of the fruit as you and I and will compete for the berries even before fully ripened. Fortunately, I usually have a couple of cats who enjoy nothing quite so much as sitting in the sun waiting for the first bird or squirrel to carelessly wander within range. I have lost few berries to these pests. Other deterrents to these pests are netting, which is most effective against the birds, and frequent picking. I have never had an insect problem. Another problem during the bearing season if the weather is unusually wet, is mildew. Spraying with a recommended fungicide is helpful under these circumstances.

Once production is over the plants will begin to send out runners—your next year's plants. At this time, cut the tops off the parent plants to encourage these runners. When the runners are about a foot long they will stop growing in length and begin to develop leaves and roots. A stone placed on the stem of the runner near the roots will keep the plant where you want it and keep the roots in contact with the soil. Nature will do the rest. When well established in the fall, "cut the cord" from the parent plant. A covering of leaves, straw, pine needles or other mulch should be used to cover the plants during the very cold winter months. This should be removed in early spring when the first signs of sprouting are noticed.

RASPBERRIES

As kids (there were six of us) my brothers, sisters and I were expected to work to help supplement the family income. One job we remember that was not too strenuous a chore with "benefits" was picking raspberries for a local grower. We went by the old rule: "one for the bucket, one for the mouth." And we all became devoted to this not too common but uncommonly good fruit. Now, during the bearing season, my whole family can be found, at some time or another, in my raspberry patch.

I got my plants from a friend, but they are available through catalogs or your local nursery. The varieties most often chosen by local farmers as being successful in this area are: *Heritage* (everbearing), *Taylor* (July-bearing), and *Newburgh* (July-bearing). The variety in my garden is *Heritage,* and they produce well twice during the summer. Since we do not use these berries for jam, it is nice to have the everbearing produce later in the season when the other berries are done.

Raspberries like full sun and well-drained soil. Plant in early spring about two feet apart in rows at least four feet apart if you plan to tie your plants. If you prefer to allow them to bush out, rows six to eight feet apart are necessary. For the family production, one row about fifty feet long should be adequate. Work some organic matter into the soil as you are planting.

During the first year, allow the plants to grow. You can let them bush out, but I have found after years of experience that tying them works best. They are easier to cultivate, prune, and harvest.

During the second year and every year thereafter, cut bushes back to 4 feet in early spring. Where necessary, remove all frost damaged portions of each stalk. The remaining good stalks will produce in late June and July. The new shoots that appear after pruning will produce your second crop in late August and September. After harvesting your first crop, remove the old growth which has finished bearing to allow proper development of the new growth.

My raspberries have caused me very little trouble in the way of pests or problems. I fertilize them in the early spring with manure, but I am sure any good quality fertilizer will work. Again, for mildew I use a fungicide.

GRAPES

The Mid-Hudson Valley is particularly kind to grapes. Most of the vines in my vineyard were planted by my father more than 60 years ago. Though age, disease, and an occasionally frisky plow horse have caused the loss of some vines over the years, grapevines are sturdy, long-lasting, and easy to propagate. In fact, you should be able to obtain the plants you want locally—from a grower or a friend—with small rooted vines or cuttings.

In our family the grapes were grown for sale to a local juice plant. The grapes we did not sell we would process for wine. Come early fall, we'd all set aside a few days to pick and pack grapes, then grind and press the excess grapes. The juice would be strained into waiting barrels, sugar added and the fermentation process begun. After a few weeks of waiting, we'd sneak down to "check on the wine" even though we knew it wasn't ready. Green wine (half-fermented juice) is an elusive treat of short duration.

Of course, homemade grape jelly is a favorite of most folks, and the juice of the grapes we grow can also be canned for future use. The two varieties most suited to this area are *Concord* and *Niagara,* with *Delaware* found occasionally in local vineyards. All these varieties are good eating, but you will find them different from the California eating grapes sold in area supermarkets.

As with the other small fruits, vines can be purchased. They are, however, so easy to propagate that you should try to obtain cuttings or even rooted vines if you know of someone with a small vineyard. If you are able to get cuttings in the early spring, root them in a bucket of damp sand. Should you be near a pond or stream, you can also sink them into the soft, moist soil near the water's edge. Mark them, though; one year I almost lost them when warm weather brought lush vegetation to the area. Once well-rooted, plant vines in soil in which you have worked organic matter.

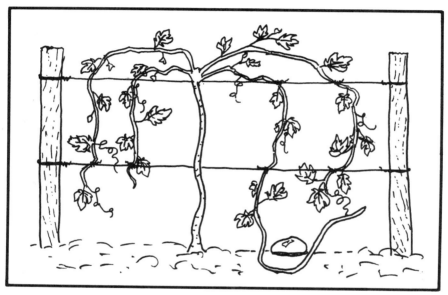

7-3 Rooting new shoot from existing vine.

To root plants on existing vines, take a long shoot in the early spring (one which would usually be pruned back) and allow it to drop to the ground. Bury the portion of this shoot where it touches the ground and weight it to keep it under the ground (diagram 7-3). By the following spring this will be a well-established vine ready to be cut from its "mother" and moved if so desired. This is the surest method of propagation and the one I prefer.

In my opinion, the most crucial step in the cultivation of grapes is the pruning. During the first year of growth and every year thereafter, the vines must be properly pruned and tied to assure healthy limbs with maximum production. I set my vines between posts to which heavy wires have been attached at a comfortable picking level (chest level and waist level). During the first year of growth, you will select one sturdy-looking limb to be the supporting limb; tie this to the wires and remove all other suckers. The following winter, cut this back to the top wire (diagram 7-4). During the second year, new growth will appear. Remove all but two of the most productive-looking limbs from the top. Thereafter, during each winter select only four limbs to remain on each vine for bearing. They can be pruned and tied in either of the two methods shown in Diagram (7-5).

7-4 Pruning first year grape vine.

Let me define a productive-looking limb. It should be at least the diameter of a pencil. The buds on this limb should be fat and close together. During the first producing season, keep only two such limbs (approximately 20 buds); and every year thereafter keep four (approximately 40 buds). I prune my vines during the winter months when the plants are dormant. Choose "warm" winter days—They will be more comfortable for you and healthier for the vines (less freeze-back).

Once spring arrives the vines will need to be fertilized and cultivated regularly. I keep the entire length of each row free of weeds well out from each vine. Fortunately, with a horse and plow, I am able to cultivate right up to the roots without damaging the plant. With a tiller you should be able to do the same. By hand this could be quite a chore and you may find that keeping the weeds clear at the base of each vine is adequate. Also during spring and summer, I strip the vine of suckers so that its energy goes into the limbs. Thereafter, the possible problems you might have are rot, which can be treated with a fungicide, or saw worm which is controlled with an application of a recommended insecticide.

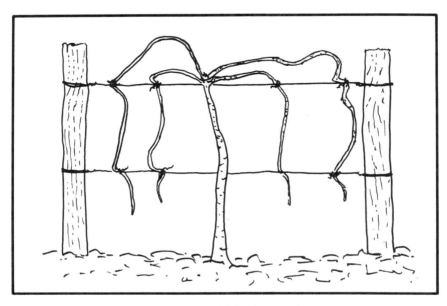

7-5 Pruning established grape vine.

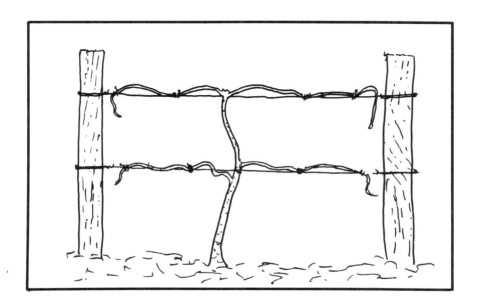

During the summer, the only job you will have is keeping suckers off the producing vines and the weeds away from the plants. Once fall arrives, you can tell your grapes are ready to pick by sampling them. They will always be ready by October 1. When we pick we use heavy-duty shears, although my sister has a knack for snapping the bunches off the vines easily and quickly.

FIGS

Although not too many folks raise figs, I'll mention them briefly, as we have raised them for years, and they are a delicious fresh fruit—not at all like the dried version in the stores. Because they cannot tolerate freezing temperatures, they must be raised in large pots and require more care than plants indigenous to the area.

The pots I use for my fig trees are halves of 50 gallon wine barrels. Any large container will do. Two things must be done before adding the tree and soil—holes for drainage should be drilled near the bottom and a dolly should be made to fit under it for ease of moving. After that you can plant your tree in a good quality soil with plenty of organic matter to help retain moisture. As far as obtaining fig trees, you may find them in nurseries or may order them through nurseries. I occasionally propagate new trees to sell or give to friends, so if you know of someone with a tree, you might ask for a cutting.

Fig trees should winter in cool, dark places like a basement or attached garage where the proximity of your home keeps temperatures above freezing. As spring approaches, I roll my trees out into the sun on those days when frost is not a threat and return them to safety in the late afternoon. Once frost is no longer a possibility, you can leave your trees out 24-hours a day. I choose a spot that receives sun all day.

As potted plants dry out quickly, you should water fig trees daily. Fertilize in the spring during the development of leaves and fruit with a mild fertilizer such as that used for house plants (I use Miracle-gro). Fruit is ready when it is large, soft, and starts to wilt. This is usually late July, August, and September, depending on the weather.

Once production is over, leave your tree out until the frost hits and sends the sap back into the roots (December 1 is a good date for this area). The tree will have lost its foliage and is now ready to trim. You must trim these trees to keep them in a size that can be handled as a potted plant and to encourage branching. The more branches, the more fruit. As figs are borne on new growth, trimming back each year is essential for production. After pruning, your tree is ready to move inside to sleep until next year.

7-6 Mobile fig tree.

8

Let's Grow Tree Fruit

By Steve Clark

In general all deciduous fruits can be grown in the Hudson Valley. Apples, pears, peaches, cherries, plums, nectarines, and even apricots can be successfully grown in Dutchess County. However, not all of these crops can be grown in all parts of the area. The answer to that riddle is to evaluate your site for low winter temperatures and potential for spring frost. The pome buds will withstand temperatures to -30°F. The stone fruit group; cherries, peaches, plums, nectarines, and apricots, are quite sensitive to temperatures below -10°F.

CHOOSING YOUR SITE

If you made a thermal map of your property you might see variations in temperature. If you have a slope, the top of the hill is generally warmer than the valley on the cold, calm nights when frost or cold temperature are a problem. If you live near a large lake or river this can temper the surrounding area delaying bloom in the spring to escape frosts. I should explain the difference between freeze and frost. Freeze damage will take place during the winter dormant period and either kill or damage the fruit buds. Frost injury is confined to the period leading up to and after bloom. At the point of full bloom most flowers will be killed at temperatures below 27°F! If the top of the hill is 29°F, and the bottom is 25°F this becomes a significant factor.

The point should be taken that if your site is not suitable because of either freeze or frost, you condemn yourself to failure by planting fruit trees on it. If you have determined your site to be acceptable in relation to temperature, then we must next look at the soil. It is best if it is fairly deep, (four feet or better), and well drained. None of the fruit trees will do well on soil that is saturated, for the roots have little available oxygen. Most soils can be drained if they are too wet. Shallow and droughty, (sandy or gravelly), soils can be irrigated to overcome those deficiencies. The pH of the soil should be between 5.5 and 6.5. This can be corrected by the addition of ground limestone if the pH is below 5.5. With the amount of acid rain we have in the East I don't believe we have any alkaline soils over pH 7.0 that will be a problem. Soils that are low in pH tie up the elements so they are unavailable for tree growth. I think now we can do some serious planning for the orchard!

PLANNING THE ORCHARD

I am going to suggest you give yourself a full year to plan and prepare the site. Fruit growing is a long term commitment and mistakes are not easily corrected, so it is much better to get it right the first time. Most fruits need at least two different varieties so that cross pollination and fertilization can take place. Not all varieties bloom at the same time, and it may be necessary to have a third variety so there can be two varieties in bloom at all times.

I would also like to suggest in your planning you try to pick apple rootstocks which will give you an 8' - 12' tree. I will cover those choices a little further on.

The most frost free site should be given over to the stone fruits. The apricots bloom first and should only be attempted in well-protected, frost free sites. I have seen trees in bloom in the Hudson Valley the first week of April. Cherries are the next most frost prone fruit and should also be on high ground. Peaches and nectarines suffer most of their bud loss in the winter. If there are several warm days and nights in the winter peaches will lose their cold hardiness, and a sudden cold snap will kill all the buds. They tend to be quite hardy during bloom and will suffer some frost. Prunes and plums will be the hardiest of the stone fruits. Apples and pears, the pome fruits, do suffer winter damage, but it is not normally as total as in the stone fruits. Their greatest danger is at bloom time, when 27 °F can be fatal.

If you have enough space, it is generally easier to plant the trees in rows to facilitate working them. It is also best to group the different species together as there are some differences in their management.

Some of the best planning guides are the commercial fruit catalogues from the major nurseries. Most of them are free for the asking, and I will give you their addresses. The most informative catalogue comes from the New York State Fruit Testing Cooperative Association in Geneva, New York 14456. A membership in the organization is $5.00, and you can be a cooperator to field test new varieties of fruits, grapes and berries from their breeding program.

Other good choices are:

Hilltop Orchards and Nurseries
P.O. Box 143 60397 C.R. 681
Hartford, Michigan 49057

C & O Nursery
1700 N. Wenatchee Ave.
P.O. Box 116
Wenatchee, Washington 98801

Columbia Basin Nursery
P.O. Box 458
Quincy, Washington 98848

Adams County Nursery
P.O. Box 108
Aspers, Pennsylvania 17304

As you research the catalogues you will find many more choices than you ever thought possible. Apples and peaches that mature from July to October; historical varieties that are no longer commercially available; apples that are disease resistant; which stone fruits are most winter hardy. Then there are all the rootstock choices. It will take a year just to sort it all out! I will make some suggestions on varieties here, but don't limit yourself to my choices.

RECOMMENDED VARIETIES

Apples

Paulared	Hilltop Nursery, late August, large, easy to grow, fairly disease free.
Jonamac	Early September, very productive, good flavor, not too large a tree.
Spartan	Mid-September, small apples, if not properly thinned, very disease resistant. I would recommend a dwarfing rootstock for this vigorous tree.
Empire	This will be New York's premier apple. Has to be well thinned for size, should be on a medium size rootstock, excellent flavor.
Jonagold	Early October, outstanding flavor and good size; very popular in Europe where fruit is chosen for flavor.
Mutsu	A Japanese import! Vigorous tree that needs dwarfing rootstock. Very large crisp fruit. Pollen is infertile.
Ida Red	Mid-October, very productive, needs to be thinned and fertilized, fairly small tree. Fruit will store in garage or cellar for several months.
Law Strain Rome	Mid-October, the redeeming grace of this apple is that it blooms very late and will produce in frosty sites. It is also self-fertile and can be planted alone. A beautiful red apple.
Granny Smith	I can't recommend this apple because it will not mature in our area. Try it if you like, but it requires a 180 day growing season from bloom until harvest.
Macintosh, etc.	Other varieties that will perform well in our area include the familiar Macintosh, Red Delicious and Cortland.

Apricot: In general I will recommend varieties from the Canadian program because of their cold hardiness.

Alfred — Mid-July, self-fruitful, bloom has some frost resistance and is quite productive.

Hargrand — Mid-July, very large fruit, tree is hardy, productive, with some disease resistance.

Harogem — Mid-late July, excellent keeping quality, small to medium fruit, very productive.

Peaches: I will again choose the most cold hardy varieties. They are also some of the best tasting.

Harbinger — Early-mid July, small size, moderately hardy, good for an early season peach.

Harken — Mid-late July, medium size fruit, fairly hardy tree, not overly vigorous.

Newhaven — Early August, appears to be slightly better than Red Haven, cold hardy and a good cropper that sizes well.

Harrow Beauty — Late August, large, attractive fruit; medium vigor and productive.

Elberta — Early September, still a good productive late season peach.

Sweet Sue — Hilltop Nursery: late September, fruit is large and tree is strong and hardy.

Nectarines: These have had problems with brown rot disease as the fruit matures and will have to be sprayed to control this disease. All nectarines are self-fruitful and do not cross pollinate.

Harko — Early-mid August; hardy, with good size if thinned.

Independence — Mid-August, very hardy blossoms, large fruit.

Nectared 6   Late August, hardy blossoms, medium-sized fruit.

Japanese Plums: These are the large oval plums that you buy from California in the summer. The trees require cross pollination so two different varieties must be set.

New York 1502   Mid-July, unnamed from Geneva, medium sized, early.

Shiro   Early August, very hardy, oversets and must be hand thinned for good size.

Santa Rosa   Early August, developed by Burbank in California, not totally winter hardy, large fruit that keeps well.

European Plums: These are generally the blue, oblong, prune type plums. They are more winter hardy than the Japanese plums.

Mount Royal   Hilltop Nursery, dwarfish tree that is very hardy.

Stanley   Late August, excellent for canning and eating, winter hardy.

Empress   Hilltop Nursery, mid-September, late productive and large.

Green Gage   Mid-September, dating from before 1699 in Europe. Still a very high quality plum.

French Damson   Early-mid September, small tart plum used in jams. This is one your grandparents would have used!

Sweet Cherry: Anyone who has a cherry tree knows about birds. You grow and they pick. I will reveal a system to foil them later on.

Ulster	Mid-late June, a New York introduction, moderately winter hardy, big beautiful cherries that hang well on the tree for over a week at maturity.
Stella	Late June, this is the only good, self-fertile sweet cherry. So if you only want one, this is it.
Ranier	Mid-late June, this is my recommendation for a good, light colored cherry. This is the one to can. It does not take rain without splitting, so some years will be a bust, but that's farming!
Hedelfingen	Early July, one of the best here and in Europe.

Sour or Tart Cherry: These trees are very hardy and will grow almost anywhere. They are self-fertile and require little care. We all know about tart cherry pie, but have you ever tried the juice as a mixer or dried tart cherries.

Montmorency	Early-mid July. This is the standard strain for the industry.
Galaxy	Hilltop Nurseries; new strain of Montmorency with a smaller, more open, tree.

Pears: These fruits, like peaches and nectarines will ripen off the tree to their full flavor. When ripe, most pears have a soft texture and are not crisp. The biggest problem you are likely to encounter with pears is fireblight, a bacterial disease. When it strikes, the branches will look like a blowtorch burned them!

Bartlett	Late August, the best canning pear and very good to eat.
Buerre Bosc	Mid-September, an excellent dessert pear that stores very well.

Seckel	Early-mid September. These small pears are a gourmet's delight when ripe. Small bundles of nectar.
Red Sensation	Early September. This is a red strain of Bartlett and the color is stable. The leaves have a reddish cast and they are less vigorous because of this, but the fruit is a beautiful crimson color.

ROOTSTOCKS

Now that we have covered some of the varieties I will further complicate the equation with rootstocks. One of your goals as a gardener is to plan the orchard so it can be maintained from the ground as much as possible. The apricot, peach, nectarine, plum and prune trees can be trained to an open center system which I will cover in the pruning section. The only choice of rootstock will be with apples, and we will confine our discussion to those. The choices I will suggest are:

Malling IX	This is a full dwarf tree and it must be supported on either a trellis or a 2" - 3" stake about 8' tall. Most trees will produce fruit in the second or third year, and the tree will almost stop growing. It is shallow rooted and may need irrigation. The tree must grow well the first two years it is in the ground or it will be a runt.
Malling 26	This needs good soil and some staking the first three years. It is a good productive rootstock that should give you an 8' - 12' tree.
Malling VIIa	This is an excellent choice for most varieties. It tends to lose its central leader if not pruned hard, and the tree will become a bush. That may not be all bad as it will keep the tree height lower.

MM III   I would use this for sites that are droughty or have shallow soil. Normally it will produce a 15' - 20' tree, but under poor conditions will probably be the correct choice.

Read the information you have collected and try to couple a weak growing tree like *Empire* or *Ida Red* with a moderate to strong rootstock like *Malling VII* or *MM III*. A strong grower like *Macintosh* or *Jonagold* should go on *Malling 26*.

Most of the trees should be spaced 15' - 20' apart. The exception will be trees planted on *Malling IX*. These trees will be 6' - 8' tall and only 8' apart, but they will have to be supported. All of the stone fruits can also be planted in the 15' - 20' spacing.

Now you can order your trees. Try to have them delivered in early April by UPS service. When they come make sure they stay in a cool place until they are planted.

PREPARING THE SITE

The spring and summer before the trees come is the time to prepare the site. If it's wet, drain it; if the pH is low, lime it! Mark out the rows the September or October before and mark the tree sites. The sod should be removed in a 3' circle around where the tree will go. This can be done with a contact herbicide like Roundup or with a shovel. Trees do much better when they do not have to compete with grass and weeds.

PLANTING

Make sure before you plant that the soil is not too wet; other than that the sooner the better. Dig the hole wide enough to hold the roots and deep enough so that the graft union between variety and rootstock is one inch above ground. No higher and no lower! After planting prune the tree back to 30" - 36" for apple and pear and cherry and 24" - 30" for the rest. This will help bring the top of the tree back into balance with some of the root surface lost in shipping. ¼ # of 10-10-10 can also be spread over the cleared area where the tree is planted. It would be a good idea to mulch that 3' circle to keep the weeds down and moisture in the ground.

TRAINING AND PRUNING

I would like to make some general comments about training and pruning that will help you understand the tree's reaction to pruning. Let me define training as the pruning cuts that help you create the type of tree structure that you desire. After creating that structure, pruning thins out the extra wood and maintains the structure. You will find that fruit spurs will weaken and produce smaller fruit after three or four years of fruiting. These can be removed individually or a whole branch can be removed, and another allowed to grow and replace it. Dormant pruning is a growth stimulating process and summer pruning will slow growth. Summer pruning should be done only on apples, between July 15 and September 1. It involves cutting out the growth initiated since the spring of the year. It should be restricted to mature, fruiting trees. Dormant pruning should consist of renewing spurs by whole branch removal and cutting the top to the height you wish to hold. If the trees fruit well this should not be too difficult. I will recommend a central leader system for apples, pears and cherries. The rest of the fruit trees should be trained to open center system.

The central leader system (8-1) consists of a central leader growing straight up, with three whorls of laterals growing out from it. These whorls consist of four branches each at ninety degree angles to each other. The first one is between 30" - 36" from the ground. The second should be 36" or so above the first and the third 24" - 36" above the second. The bottom whorl should attain a length of 5' - 7'; the second whorl 3' - 5'; and the top whorl 1' - 3'. The result should be an 8' - 12' tree that tapers like a lampshade so that the bottom branches have as much sunlight as the top. The branches should be physically placed at a sixty to seventy-five degree angle from the central leader to promote fruiting. These branches tend to grow up toward the sun and a brick or other appropriate weight tied to the branch will bring it to the desired angle.

The open center tree (8-2) does just the opposite. Choose three branches for laterals spaced about 120° apart. They should be spaced 3" - 4" apart vertically on the trunk to give the crotch strength. The upright sprouts should be removed to force the growth in these laterals in a horizontal manner. If they became too upright they can also be pulled down with a weight. These bloom and fruit their second year. After they have fruited, simply remove them and this year's suckers will carry next year's crop. Try not to let the stone fruits in this system ever get over 8', or it will become too shaded and the crop will move higher up the tree. If this happens just cut it back and start all over again from your three branch framework. Peaches and nectarines need to be heavily pruned after they come into production. Only the shoots 1/8" and larger should be used for fruiting and these can be cut back to four or five buds. Even after this you will have to remove 60% - 70% of the fruits to achieve size on the remaining 30% - 40%.

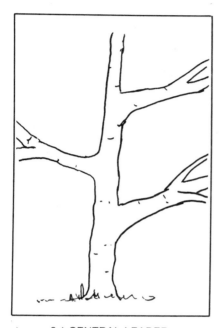

8-1 CENTRAL LEADER

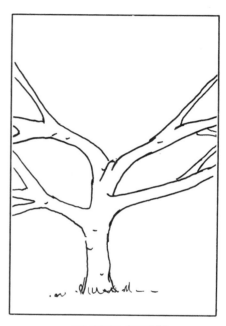

8-2 OPEN CENTER

The dormant pruning on the pome fruits can begin anytime after January first. Cherries and plums can be pruned in March and April. Delay pruning apricots, peaches and nectarines until just before or during bloom. There is a disease called Valsa Canker which will infect cuts made in cold weather. You can escape the disease by simply pruning in warm weather.

INSECT AND DISEASE CONTROL

This is always a difficult subject to discuss with a general audience, so I will provide a very minimal program assuming you are willing to trade a full chemical control program for some insect and disease damage.

I will take the stone fruit first because they have a simpler program. Until they crop, their only problem will be with aphids and peach tree borer. The aphids will transmit viruses and must be controlled when you see colonies building up. Peach tree borers lay their eggs in the butts of the trees, and the larvae from these eggs eat the wood and bark of the trees and can girdle them. They attack all stone fruits as well as dogwoods. A drench spray from waist high to the soil line will eliminate this pest. Our biggest problem with all the stone fruits is brown rot. As the fruit begins to ripen and soften this fungus can infect the whole crop. It has to rain at fairly warm temperatures for the spores to be released and infect the fruit, but this is quite common. To control the disease a fungicide has to be on the fruit before it rains or within 24 hours from the beginning of the rain.

The pome fruits have several more problems to contend with, but most of the problems can be controlled with minimal application of chemicals if the timing is correct. Controlling aphids until the trees fruit should be adequate for young trees. The orange larvae of the lady bug will sometimes control colonies of aphids, and if this biological contol is working, I would not attempt chemical control. When the trees begin to produce fruit a more complete program will be needed to protect the fruit. A 2% emulsifiable oil spray should be applied when the new fruit blossoms are in a tight, green cluster. Just before the earliest blooms burst open, an insecticide and fungicide should be applied. During bloom and for two to three weeks after will be the heaviest amount of apple scab spore discharge. These spores are only discharged during rainy periods. The apples should be covered during this time with a fungicide renewed every seven to ten days. Do not use any insecticide when the blooms are open! It may be fatal to the bees. A second insecticide can be applied after all the bloom is off and the third applied in mid-July. That should do it. If you have serious problems with insects or diseases call you county extension service and ask for help.

NOTES ON APPLES

The most serious problem you will encounter with apples is fruit thinning. Apples are naturally biennial; they bloom and crop heavily one year, and have no bloom on the alternate year. Commercial fruit growers overcome this by applying Napthalene Acetic Acid to the tree 14 - 21 days after full bloom. On many varieties the insecticide Sevin or Carbaryl will do a similar job if applied at the same time. I would suggest its use as the petals fall; spray to control insects as well as thin the fruit. The more dwarfing rootstocks will help overcome this biennial tendency also, by being more precocious. For optimum size of fruit, I will suggest hand thinning in July to a spacing of one fruit every 6". Another surprise you will encounter will be "June drop". A fruit tree will naturally shed a portion of the crop it has set; and these fruits will drop in June. Don't be alarmed; the tree is trying to adjust to what its chemical sensors say it can carry. If you have limited room for apples, plant one variety, and later graft others onto it. This also solves the cross pollination problem.

NOTES ON PEARS

Pears are slower to mature than apples and are not as productive. They should also be thinned at least to a single fruit per spur. If the trees become infected with Fire Blight, cut below the infected branch and rinse the clippers between every cut with alcohol to prevent spreading. Burn the prunings.

NOTES ON CHERRIES

Don't let the tree get too large. They respond well to heavy pruning, so keep them to 12'. BIRDS! Birds begin to attack the fruit when it changes to a reddish color and will clean the trees long before the fruit is ripe. If the trees are no taller than 12' it is quite easy to cover with plastic netting. This will allow enough light to penetrate and ripen the crop and the birds will become confused when they fly into the tree.

NOTES ON APRICOTS, PEACHES, PLUMS AND PRUNES

These will have to be thinned and pruned hard. If they are maintained at 8' it is much easier to work on them. With peaches and nectarines, try and thin to one fruit every 3" - 4". The butts of all the trees should be painted with white latex paint to prevent southwest injury. During clear, sunny days in winter, the sun can warm the bark of the tree and force sap to move up it. After the sun drops in the southwest, the air temperature can plummet and the tree cannot respond quickly enough. The sap freezes and kills the bark. The white paint will reflect some of the sunlight and the bark will stay much cooler and not split.

LET'S GROW!

I hope I have not discouraged you too much. The beauty and fragrance of the blossoms at bloom are well worth the planning and work involved. There is no describing the flavor of tree ripened fruit at the peak of ripeness. You will encounter many problems I have not talked about. I will refer you to the extension agent in your county for advice in solving them. I hope you spend many enjoyable hours planning and tending your orchard.

9

Let's Landscape

By Carl Norton

There are great variations of soil types in Dutchess County, ranging from sandy gravel to heavy shale soil high in clay content that is, especially in dry seasons, almost impossible to dig by hand. Because of these conditions, it becomes very important when planting in Dutchess to give your plants the best possible soil preparation.

One thing in our favor is that the nutrient levels in even the poorest looking soil is usually fine for supporting home landscape planting, so it comes down to conditioning properly with generous amounts of organic materials like peat moss, peat humus, or leaf mould. As a general practice mix 1 (4 cu. foot) bale of peat moss with each ½ cu. yard of soil. Use more if your soil is very heavy.

When conditioning your soil for planting, mix in a light fertilizer at the same time. New plantings cannot use high nitrogen fertilizer until after they are established or acclimated to the site, so it's a waste of time and money to apply them during planting. A very convenient method of fertilizing new plantings is to use slow release fertilizer packs. They are small, water soluble packets of slow release particles that break down over three years to supply the plant with nutrients as it can use them. As I've stated earlier, plants grow very well in Dutchess soils so that unless a plant is off color, with noticeable deficiencies, it's not necessary to fertilize (especially foundation plantings, as the increased growth will become an increased pruning and maintenance problem).

FOUNDATION PLANTINGS

When planting close to your house use dwarf or compact grow-ing plants. It may seem as if they will take forever to grow and fill in, but you'll be surprised how quickly it happens. With the proper design and by investing a bit more for the expensive plants, you can extend the life of your new foundation plantings by 10-20 years or longer.

If planting a small tree in your foundation planting, keep it 8-10' away from the building. Small trees like Red bud, Japanese tree lilac, or Kousa dogwood, need at least that much room for head development.

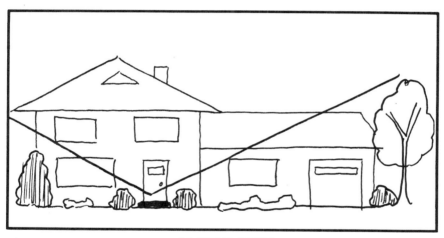

9-1 FOCAL POINT

When planning the design of your foundation planting, arrange your plants to show direction to a focal point like the front door, (diagram 9-1) or a walk, or a special feature of your house.

Avoid planting foundation plants tightly across the house. It gives the impression that the building is floating on a sea of green with no connection to the ground.

GROUPINGS

Always avoid using many different varieties of plants in small areas. It creates a busy, jumbled appearance, whereas groupings of the same varieties of plants create a soothing appearance. Along a house that is 50' long, I would use no more than five varieties. I would also suggest that you use the same type of plant at intervals throughout the length of the planting to create continuity or to tie the plantings together.

When you think of planting, it's very important to know how large your favorite plant grows. For instance, if spacing of border plants (flowering shrubs) is incorrect, they will suffer from reduced flowers, erratic or stunted growth, and shading of lower branches. In time they would become an overall jungle that would have to be cleaned out with a chain saw. For example, a full grown Weigela can be 12-14' tall and 10-12' across, or a Deutzia that is 3-4' tall will be 4-5' across the base. As a general rule, plant flowering shrubs their mature height apart or a minimum of 8' on center.

If density is your goal (for screening), plant flowering shrubs or evergreens in a double staggered row. (Diagram 9-2) It looks natural and becomes very dense.

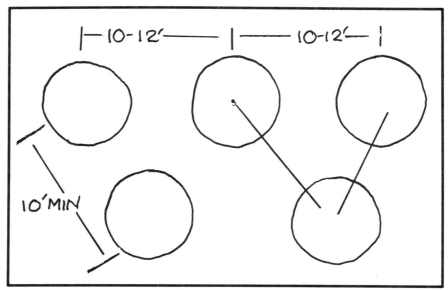

9-2 Double Staggered row planting

Large plants like shade and evergreen trees can grow to over 100' and require more space for development.

For planting along a driveway or street, plant maple, locust or oak, a minimum of 40' on center.

As a final thought on landscape design--when you create an outdoor living space or room, think of the grass as the floor, tree trunks as the walls and the tree canopy of branches as the ceiling.

HARDINESS

There is such a great variation of temperature in Dutchess County that a plant that grows well in one may have little or no chance in another. The Hudson River has a great warming effect for a half to one mile in along its banks, and tender or marginal plants can be grown in this area with fair to good success. Likewise, from north to south along the Hudson there are considerable variations in temperature, and an American holly planted in Beacon has a much better chance than the same plant does in Tivoli. There are exceptions to these generally accepted rules, and as proof of this, if you drive north on Route 9G toward Rhinebeck and turn left on Violet Hill Road, you can see the most beautiful stand of American Holly that you would want to see anywhere. Obviously this is a micro-climate and not typical of the area, and I'm not suggesting that it's o.k. to plant American holly in Rhinebeck. My only point is that a lot of variation does exist.

The same condition exists for semi-evergreen azaleas. They can be found growing in micro-climates around the county but are generally not hardy for Dutchess. Some other plants in this category are boxwood, Japanese holly, mahonia, sweet gum, and golden chain.

It's important when you do landscape planting in Dutchess or any other county, to select low maintenance, disease resistant, hardy plants, so that you're not disappointed later after you've invested time and money. It would be impractical to try to list all the trees and shrubs that are low maintenance in our area; however, there are a few that I consider exceptionally good:

> Amelanchier canadensis (shadblow)
> Cotinus coggygria (smokebush)
> Euonymus Alatus compactus (burning bush)
> Viburnum prunifolium (black haw viburnum)
> Cercidiphyllum japonica (katsura tree)

Likewise there are some plants that I consider high maintenance, and among them are: disease problems with crab-apple, hawthorn and mt. ash; chlorosis on pin oak (loss of green color); and more recently, anthracnose disease on dogwood and dieback on Japanese andromeda.

If you have a dogwood tree that's showing symptoms of anthracnose (lower branch dieback with, or yellowing of lower leaves), the best treatment is to keep it as healthy as possible, well fertilized, watered during dry spells; prune dead wood and apply a fungicide.

If Japanese andromeda or rhododendron are planted in sunny areas, you can expect to have lace wing fly damage. This shows up as a mottled effect on the leaves. You will have to spray for these insects. When the same plants are planted in semi-shady areas, they are seldom troubled with lace wing fly.

When planting shade trees in Dutchess County, it is very important to guy the trees and wrap the trunks. Guying prevents the trunk from loosening in the root ball and damaging the root system. It also keeps the trunk and tree head straight. Wrapping the trunk helps prevent sun scald on the tender bark of a newly planted tree. Sun scald is caused by winter sun heating the southern side of a young tree trunk. Shortly thereafter extreme temperature fluctuation causes the green cambium under the bark to die and the bark to separate up and down the trunk. Wrapping newly planted trees with kraft paper or burlap tree wrap will help prevent sun scald.

SHRUBS FOR DUTCHESS COUNTY

Amelanchier Canadensis	(Shadbush)	25'
Berberis Thunbergi	(Barberry)	6'
Buddleia Davidi	(Butterfly Bush)	12 - 14'
Calluna Vulgaris	(Heather)	12 - 18''
Calycanthus Floridus	(Carolina Allspice)	6 - 9'
Caragana Arborescens	(Siberian Pea-tree)	18'
Caryopteris Clandonensis	(Bluemist)	3 - 4'
Chaenomeles Japonica	(Japanese Quince)	3 - 4'
Chamaecyparis Obtusa Varieties	(Hinoki Cypress)	
Chionanthus Virginicus	(Fringe Tree)	30'
Clethra Alnifolia	(Summersweet)	6 - 8'
Cornus Alba Sibirica	(Red Twig Dogwood)	8 - 9'
Cornus Mas	(Cornelian Cherry)	24'
Corylus Contorta	(Lauders Walking Stick)	12 - 14'
Cotinus Coggygria	(Smoke Tree)	15'
Cotoneaster Varieties	(Cotoneaster)	
Cytisus Scoparius	(Scotch Broom)	6'
Daphne Cneorum	(Rose Daphne)	6''
Deutzia Gizacilis	(Slender Deutzia)	3 - 5'
Elaeagnus Angustiflia	(Russian Olive)	20'
Enkianthus Campanulatus	(Redvein Enkianthus)	
Epigaea Repens	(Trailing Arbutus)	Ground Cover
Erica Varieties	(Heath)	18 - 24''
Euonymus Alata Varieties	(Spindle Tree)	9'
Euonymus Japonica Varieties [E]	(Evergreen Euonymus)	10 - 12'
Forsythia Varieties		8 - 9'
Hamamelis Virginiana	(Witch Hazel)	15'
Hibiscus Syriacus	(Shrub Althea)	
Hydrangea Varieties	(Hydrangea)	3 - 15'
Ilex Rugosa	(Blue Hollies)	
Ilex Verticillata	(Winterberry)	6 - 8'
Juniperus Varieties [E]	(Juniper)	3'' - 9'
Kalmia Angustifolia [E]	(Sheep Laurel)	3'
Kalmia Latifolia [E]	(Mountain Laurel)	12 - 15'
Kerria Japonica	(Kerria)	4 - 5'
Kolkwitzia Amabilis	(Beauty Bush)	10'
Ligustrum Amurense	(Amur Privet)	12 - 15'
Lindeiza Benzoin	(Spice Bush)	15'
Lonicera Tatarica	(Tatarian Honeysuckle)	9'
Magnolia Varieties	(Magnolia)	20 - 25'
Mitchella Repens	(Partridge Berry)	Ground Cover
Myrica Pensylvanica	(Bayberry)	10'
Paeonia Suffroticosa	(Tree Peony)	3 - 4'
Philadelphus Coronarius	(Sweet Mock Orange)	8 - 9'
Pieris Floribunda [E]	(Mountain Andromeda)	4 - 5'
Pinus Pensiflora Umbraculifera [E]	(Tanyosho Pine)	12'
Pinus Mugo Mughus [E]	(Mugo Pine)	8 - 9'
Potentilla Fruticosa	(Bush Cinquefoil)	3 - 4'
Prunus Glandulosa	(Dwarf Flowering Almond)	3 - 4'

TREES & LARGE SHRUBS HARDY AND SUITABLE
FOR AREAS AROUND MILLBROOK

Acer Ginnaca	(Amur Maple)	20'
Acer Pacmatum	Japanese Maple	20'
Acer Saccharum	(Sugar Maple)	100' +
Betula Papyrifera	(Paper Birch)	50 - 60'
Betula Pendula	(European Birch)	30 - 40'
Cercidipuyllum Japonicum	(Katsura Tree)	60 - 90'
Cercis Canadensis	(Eastern Redbud)	30'
Champecyparis Obtusa [E]	(Hinoki Cypress)	70 - 80'
Cladrostis Lutea	(Yellow Wood)	40'
Cornus Kousa	(Chinese Dogwood)	20'
Cotinus Americanus	(Smoke Tree)	30'
Crataegus Crus Galli	(Cockspur Thorn)	30'
Fagus Grandifolia	(American Beech)	90'
Fagus Sylvatica	(European Beech)	90'
Ginkgo Biloba	(Ginkgo Tree)	100' +
Gleditsia Triacanthos Inermis	(Hybrid Locust)	100' +
Gymnocladus Dioicus	(Kentucky Coffee Tree)	80'
Juniperus Chinensis [E]	(Chinese Juniper)	50' +
Juniperus Virginiana [E]	(Red Cedar)	90'
Larix Decidua	(European Larch)	100'
Magnolia Stellata	(Star Magnolia)	20'
Malus 'Species'	(Flowering Crabapple)	20 - 40'
Phellodendron Amurense	(Amur Cork Tree)	40' +
Picea Abies [E]	(Norway Spruce)	150'
Picea Glauca Densata [E]	(Black Hills Spruce)	40'
Pinus Strobus [E]	(Eastern White Pine)	100 - 150'
Pinus Umbraculifera [E]	(Tanyosho Pine)	30 - 40'
Prunus		
Pseudotsuga Taxifolia [E]	(Douglas Fir)	100' +
Pyrus Calleryana	(Bradford Callery Pear)	30'
Quercus Borealis	(Northern Red Oak)	75' +
Salix Niobe	(Golden Twig Weeping Willow)	75' +
Syringa Amurensis Japonica	(Japanese Tree Lilac)	30'
Taxus Cuspinata [E]	(Upright Japanese Yew)	50'
Thuja Occidentacis [E]	(American Arborvitae)	60'
Tilia Cordata	(Littleleaf Linden)	
Tsuga Canadensis [E]	(Canadian Hemlock)	90'
Viburnum Prunifolium	(Blackhaw Viburnum)	15'
Zelicoua Serrota	(Japanese Zelicoua)	90'

E = Evergreen

10

Let's Grow Lawns

By Stephanie Mallozzi

Lawn care need not be considered a dreaded chore as it is to many who have pursued a lush green lawn. In this chapter we'll discuss step-by-step, the basics of lawn establishment and maintenance. With patience, perserverence and a little luck, your lawn can be a prizewinner.

SOIL

This is where it all begins! Turf grows best in a soil that is slightly acidic with pH in the range of 6.0 - 6.8 (pH measures how acid or basic the soil is). To determine pH, a soil test should be taken. Many garden centers offer this service as does Dutchess County Cooperative Extension. In addition, pH test kits may be purchased at local garden centers for home testing. Once a test is completed, the result will indicate whether or not lime must be applied. Limestone is the material commonly used to raise soil pH. If the pH is too high, then sulfur is the recommended material to lower pH. In Dutchess County, our soils tend to be on the acid side, more often than not recessitating the addition of lime. Chart (10-1) is a guide for limestone amounts. This table should be used only after a soil test determines the pH. If it is not possible to take a soil test to determine pH, then this general rule may apply: if no lime has been put on in the last three years, apply 50 pounds per 1,000 square feet.

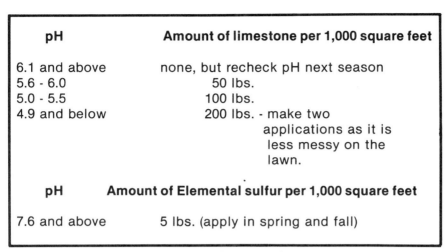

pH	Amount of limestone per 1,000 square feet
6.1 and above	none, but recheck pH next season
5.6 - 6.0	50 lbs.
5.0 - 5.5	100 lbs.
4.9 and below	200 lbs. - make two applications as it is less messy on the lawn.

pH	Amount of Elemental sulfur per 1,000 square feet
7.6 and above	5 lbs. (apply in spring and fall)

10-1 Lime and sulfer applications

Limestone may be applied in the spring or fall. Keep in mind though, lime works over the course of the season. The results are not immediate. It is applied with a lawn spreader (usually, the same one that is used for lawn fertilizer). To illustrate the value of proper pH, chart (10-2) shows nutrient availability and its effect on pH.

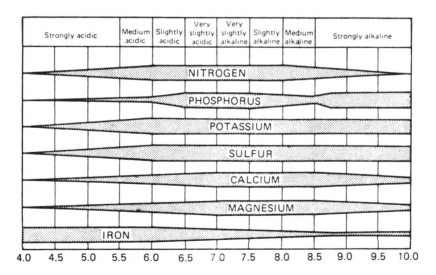

10-2 Availability of nutrients at various pH

One of the most important elements for proper turf growth is nitrogen. As illustrated in chart (10-2), it is most readily available if the pH is above 6.0. If the pH is too low or too high then essential elements are not available in a form turf plants can absorb. Therefore, pH plays a very important role in turf management.

LAWN GRASSES

Grass is grass, right? Wrong! Choosing a good lawn seed mix is a primary consideration when building or renovating a lawn. Here in Dutchess County, the recommended types fall under a category that is called "cool-season grasses". The three grass types usually recommended are a mix of: kentucky bluegrass, perennial ryegrass, and fescue. These grasses differ in their ability to tolerate various cultural conditions such as: sun, shade, drought, acidity, and traffic.

Kentucky Bluegrass: usually the major "ingredient" in a lawn mix. It is used in sunny locations. This grass has a nice medium to dark green color, a medium-textured (smooth) leaf blade, and an extensive root and rhizome (underground stem) system. Kentucky bluegrass is considered a high maintenance turf. It requires well-limed and fertilized soil. In addition, if it is not irrigated during the hot summer months, it has a tendency to turn brown and go dormant. But, usually as soon as cool, moist autumn weather returns, Kentucky bluegrass will green up again. Since Kentucky bluegrass is a high-maintenance turf type it can be more suscepti-ble to disease. Therefore when choosing varieties, look for those that are disease resistant. Some varieties of bluegrass that appear to be disease resistant and will grow well in Dutchess County in-clude:

Adelphi	Majestic	Touchdown
Bonnieblue	Enmundi	Bensun (A-34)
Flyking	Sydsport	Parade
Glade	Baron	Victa

Fine Fescues: shade and drought tolerant. They are light green in color and are very fine-textured (the leaves resemble pine needles). They do not do well in very wet locations or poorly drained soil. Fine fescues are the dominant turf type found in shady lawn seed mixtures. Some varieties include:

Banner	Highlight	Pennlawn
Biljart	Jamestown	Scaldis
Ensylva	Koket	Walding
		Waldorf

Other Grasses: two other types of grasses sometimes mentioned for home use are bentgrass and zoysia grass. Traditionally bentgrass is used on golfcourses for putting greens. It is a very high maintenance lawn grass and therefore not recommended for home lawn use.

Zoysia grass is a warm season grass. It is normally purchased and planted as "plugs" (small plants). Contrary to the advertisements, zoysia grass is not the miracle grass it claims to be. Because it is a warm-season grass, it usually does not green up until after the last frost (late September to early October). So its "green" season lasts only about six months, whereas the cool season grasses (bluegrasses, ryegrass, and fascue) will stay green for up to 10 months of the year. In certain situations where the soil is very poor, zoysia grass may be the answer. There are advantages and disadvantages to using this turf type. A few are listed below. In any case though, the choice is yours!

Advantages of zoysia grass
1. Grows well during hot summer months
2. Withstands close mowing
3. Tolerates most soil types

Disadvantages of zoysia grass

1. Loses its green color and turns straw brown after the first frost
2. Establishes slowly, over a period of 2 - 3 years
3. Once established, it is difficult to eliminate and may crowd out cool season grasses

---

10-3 Zoysia Grass

There are general guidelines for seeding mixtures. Those listed in chart (10-4) should be chosen for a specific use.

Use	Mix (% by Weight)	Lb. Mixture/1,000 sq. ft.
Sun - medium to high maintenance	55% KB blend 10-20% PR, 15% FF	3-4
Sun - low maintenance and droughty	65% FF, 10-20% PR 10-15% KB blend	4-5
Shade - dry	65% FF, 10-20% PR 10-15% shade tolerant KB blend	4-5
	or	
	80% shade tolerant KB blend, 20% PR	3-4

KB = Kentucky Bluegrass   PR = Perennial Ryegrass
FF = Fine Fescue

10-4 Grass Seed Mixtures

BUILDING A NEW LAWN

The easiest way to discuss this segment is to list a step-by-step procedure for starting a lawn from scratch. The optimum time for this operation is the period of August 15th through October 1st. Competition from weeds is usually less at this time of year and moisture is also usually more available.

- The soil should be free of twigs, debris, and stones. Grade the area (if necessary, by a bulldozer) so that it is relatively flat.

- If possible, apply four to six inches of top soil to the area. (Sometimes this is not economically feasible, and with good preparation and proper management, top soil may not be necessary).

- Have the soil tested for pH and apply lime if needed.

- If the soil is very sandy or clay, apply a layer of peat moss at the rate of three large bales per 1,000 square feet.

- Apply a complete fertilizer at the rate of two pounds of nitrogen per 1,000 square feet (example: a 10-6-4 fertilizer is 10% nitrogen, so 20 pounds of this fertilizer would contain 2 pounds of nitrogen).

- Rototill the above listed materials (topsoil, lime, peat moss, fertilizer) into the top four inches of soil.

- Rake the soil until a smooth grade is established.

- Select the proper seed mix for your soil conditions.

- Sow the seed using a spreader. Apply one half of the seed in one direction and the other half at right angles to it.

- Rake the soil lightly, just enough to barely cover the seed.

- Water the area gently, but thoroughly to keep the soil moist.

- Apply a straw mulch uniformly on the area. Usually 1-1½ bales will cover 1,000 square feet. You should be able to see at least half of the soil surface after the mulch has been applied.

- When the grass is about three inches high, start mowing. Cutting height should be two to two and a half inches.

LAWN RENOVATION

This applies to a partial seeding operation rather than starting an entire new lawn. This process improves the area by seeding into the already existing sod. If the lawn contains more than 50% desirable grasses, then renovation is called for. If there is 50% or less desirable grass, then it is better to start from scratch. The best time of year to do this is the period of August 15th - October 1st. Here are step-by-step directions for partial lawn renovation:

- To kill broadleaf weeds such as dandelion and plantain, apply a broadleaf weed killer about three weeks before the actual renovation.

- Mow the lawn to a height of ¾ inch and remove all the clippings.

- Remove thatch using a power rake.

- Core aerify the lawn. This process involves depositing plugs of soil right at the surface. It alleviates soil compaction and aerates the soil.

- Apply lime if needed (a pH test can determine this). Apply fertilizer at the rate 2 lbs. of nitrogen per 1,000 square feet. Work these materials into the soil by dragging a chain link fence across the area.

- Sow seed. Use a blend of kentucky bluegrass, fine fescue, and ryegrass. Sow one half of the seed in one direction and the other half at right angles to the first. Drag the area again to get soil-seed contact.

- Mulch the area with clean straw (1-1½ bales per 1,000 square feet).

- Moisten the area, and water other times when necessary just to moisten the surface.

- Continue to mow the rest of the lawn as usual.

LAWN MAINTENANCE

Fertilization: Lawns can be fertilized from one to five times a year. The key is not how many times you fertilize, but how much you apply. In Dutchess County, annual fertilization with two to five pounds of actual nitrogen per 1,000 square feet is recommended. Never apply more than one pound of actual nitrogen per application. The total amount of actual nitrogen you want to apply in a given year will determine how many times a year the lawn is fertilized. Use a complete fertilizer containing nitrogen, phosphorous, and potassium. If you want to apply three pounds annually, you would make three applications, two pounds, two applications, and so on. Here is a time table to follow (Chart 10-5):

Amount	Number of Application	Timing
1 lb.	1	mid-September
2 lbs.	2	mid-September and late November
3 lbs.	3	mid-September, late November and mid-May

Weed Control: This is a must for a lush and healthy green lawn. Weeds compete with desirable grasses for moisture and nutrients. Here in Dutchess County we encounter problems with many broadleaf weeds such as dandelion, plantain, and ground ivy. In addition, crabgrass, an annual grass that reproduces by seed, can also be troublesome. Crabgrass seeds can be killed by applying a crabgrass preventer in the spring, at the time the forsythia blooms begin to fade.

Broadleaf weeds are best controlled just after they begin growth in the spring. Most broadleaf weeds are perennial and therefore require a growth regulator type of herbicide to control them. This material is sprayed on the plant, absorbed, and transported down to the roots. For example, dandelion is best controlled just before the flowerheads open. The plant is actively growing at the time and will readily absorb the weed killer.

Sometimes, a weed will take over much of an area and will not die down using conventional means of control. In that case total eradication of the area is called for. The use of a non-selective weed killer such as Kleen-Up will kill everything it comes in contact with. After the area has died down it can then be reseeded.

Watering: This maintenance chore is often overlooked as a cause of turf decline, if it is neglected. Bluegrass lawns, especially, need regular irrigation. Lawns should be watered when the soil begins to dry out, but before the grass wilts and turns brown. Here in Dutchess County during the hot summer months, this could be every five days.

The turf should receive at least one inch of water a week. This can easily be measured by placing a straight-sided can or cup near the sprinkler. When the water in the container measures one inch, the sprinkler can then be moved to the next location. A light sprinkling will do more harm than good. The key to proper watering is a thorough soaking. If rainfall has been adequate during that five to seven day interval, then watering may not be necessary. If possible, water early in the morning or early in the evening, not during the heat of the day when the water may evaporate quickly and do the lawn little good.

Mowing: This chore should begin in the spring when growth resumes and end sometime in November. Basically, the lawn should be kept at the height of about two to two and a half inches. When mowing, never remove more than one third of the total leaf surface. If you mow on a regular basis leave the clippings--Yes! Leave them. They will provide nutrients and act as a mulch to conserve moisture.

Make sure the mower blades are kept sharp. A dull mower will end up shredding the leaf blades rather than making a clean cut. This can promote unwanted disease. Change directions each time you mow. In other words, mow in one direction and the next time you mow, mow at right angles or diagonally to the direction you mowed the last time. This will prevent ridges in the lawn. Avoid mowing the lawn when it is wet. This too can promote the spread of disease.

Thatch: a thick, tangled layer of dead and decaying plant parts such as stems, leaves, and roots that forms between the soil surface and grass plant. It creates an impenetratable barrier that inhibits moisture and nutrients from reaching the grass roots. In addition it can promote disease and can harbor overwintering turf insects. If thatch is present in an amount greater than three quarters of an inch, it should be removed. This is done by means of a mechanical dethatcher, which makes vertical cuts in the soil that allow air to penetrate and thus break down the thatch. This operation may be done in early spring or early fall. Do not do it in the summer.

The best way to "control" thatch is by preventing its buildup in the first place. This can be accomplished by a process called core aerification, using a machine that punches a hole in the soil, removes a core of soil and deposits it at the soil surface. This promotes aeration and increases microorganism activity which breaks down thatch.

PEST CONTROL

In this section some of the insect and disease problems prevalent in Dutchess County will be briefly discussed. No specific chemical controls will be offered. For those recommendations, it is suggested that Dutchess County Cooperative Extension be contacted.

Insects: There is definitely a top two in this category--grubs and chinch bugs!

Grubs are the immature or larvae stage of scarab beetles such as the japanese beetle. The larvae feed on tender grass roots and overwinter deep within the soil below the frost line. They are fat and wormlike with a brown head, white body and six tiny legs close to the head. When seen in the soil they are usually curled into a "C" shape. They do most of their damage in the spring and in late summer through fall. If patches of grass are browning out and you can pull healthy grass near it back like a carpet, chances are you'll find grubs below. The optimum time to control grubs is mid-summer, July through August, but they can also be controlled in the spring.

Chinch bugs are difficult to see with the naked eye. They are about one fifth of an inch long and black in color, and cause yellowing and browning of grass plants by sucking plant juices from the leaves and stems. They prefer to feed in sunny, hot areas; thus, it is most likely to see their damage June through August. To test for chinch bugs, cut out both ends of a large tin can and push one end about two inches into the soil. Fill the can with water. If chinch bugs are present, they will float to the top. If several are found, treatment is necessary. They are best controlled with an insecticide in early June with a follow-up application made two to three weeks later.

Diseases: Dutchess County usually has more insect and cultural problems than disease problems, but none the less, diseases do appear.

Leafspot is one of the more common diseases, especially during periods of cool, moist weather (spring and fall). Initially, symptoms are a spotting of the leaves. If the disease is allowed to progress, the stems and crowns of the plants will rot and die. It is important to choose leaf spot resistant grass varieties so that the incidence of this disease is reduced.

Slime mold does not affect turf grass directly, but rather indirectly. This "disease" is frequently seen following wet weather in late July or early August. A bluish gray mold can be seen on scattered areas of the lawn. It damages turf by shading the leaf blade and thus interfering with the food-making process of the plant. It is unsightly, but usually does not cause permanent damage. It is easily controlled by applying a steady stream of water or by brushing with a broom.

Small Animals: mentioned in this section because their appearance is related to insect occurrance. Skunks and moles can be found digging up the lawn or tunneling pathways through it. They are not eating the grass, but foraging for insects such as grubs or earthworms. These insects are a delicacy to these animals. The easiest way to control small animals is to control the insects! If you eliminate their food source, there's no reason for them to create havoc on your lawn.

11

Let's Not Grow Weeds

By Gary Zinsmeyer

Whether you're a city dweller with a small patch of lawn and a bit of a flower or vegetable garden or you're a county-ite with an expanse of property around your home, undesirable plants that just seem to appear spontaneously will eventually annoy you. And then, of course, even if you don't garden there's the annoyance weeds cause to us via sneezing, itchy eyes and sinus problems. By definition a weed is really any plant growing where you'd rather (for any number of reasons) have some other plant, or no plants at all. Strange as it may seem though, weeds have their good side— they prevent soil erosion. Weeds can also add considerably to the organic content of soil. And certainly weeds provide wildlife with cover and food. Weeds are nature's natural bird seed storehouse!

Historically weeds weren't here 'til we were. That's when we made judgments (based on human bias) as to what was good and what should go! Like so many other organisms, weeds are incredibly well adapted to diverse and adverse circumstances, they'll grow where not much else will— including the narrow cracks in our sidewalks and our patios. Another reason for their outstanding success survival-wise is due to their ability to produce enormous quantities of seeds — consider the dandelion. Along with seeds too numerous to ever count, many weeds can regrow, with little difficulty, a new root system after their top growth has been cut into segments. So it just goes to show you that once again man's human bias has been outwitted by mother nature!

HERBICIDES

With man's entrance into the chemical age of modern life, we've been coming up with some pretty effective materials, and ways to apply these materials, to control weeds both before and after they begin to annoy us.

Generally, herbicides, chemicals that eliminate unwanted plants, are divided into two groups. The first group called 'non-selective' is just as the term implies, killers of all or nearly all vegetation in the given area of application. The second group is called the 'selective herbicides'. These are much more sophisticated than their big brothers. We've been able to discover, through painstaking research, just how different plants live and grow. Using this information we've then perfected compounds that will kill certain plants while leaving the preferred plants unaffected. An example of a non-selective herbicide would be amitrole; a common brush killer. A selective herbicide would be any broad leafed weed killer that we use in our lawns to rid our turf of dandelions, plantain, and ground ivy— while the blue grass or fescue lawn grows on.

To take things a step or two further we can divide the selective and non-selective herbicides into two more divisions. This time we'll divide the herbicides not according to what they control but by when they're applied to control our undesirable plants. Thus these new compounds are called pre-emergence and post-emergence herbicides. Believe it or not, you can kill a weed (rather it's seed) before it gets growing and becomes a nuisance. Such a pre-emergence herbicide would be the crab grass preventers you apply to your lawn in early spring before the crab grass seeds germinate. There are also pre-emergence herbicides you can apply to your newly planted annual flower bed each spring— again to control the eventual weed problems you'd face otherwise. As a rule of thumb remember that once a pre-emergence is applied, it is then watered in. And after that, no further disturbance of the soil should occur, or else the protective weed stopping barrier would be broken.

Now that you know what's available it's important for you to understand the forms in which these weed-stopping wonders are available. Formulations, as they're known, range from granules, to concentrated liquids (you dilute and spray on), to aerosol spray cans (mixture and applicator all in one), to pre-mixed solutions in trigger spray bottles, to wax bars (containing a concentration of herbicide) you drag over the weeds, to even hollow plastic canes filled with herbicide solutions you apply in a spearing like action.

No matter what form you choose, the manufacturers of such products have gone to excessive lengths to give you exceptionally thorough directions on how best to use their products. Following the directions to the letter is the only way to use any formulation of any herbicide! Always, always measure and never, never use more than called for. If you'll be using your own equipment to spray on or disperse the mixture be sure you thoroughly clean the equipment immediately after use. Better yet if you can afford a separate set of equipment for applying herbicides— buy it! Even the slightest residue can cause damage to your preferred plants. And, if you use the same equipment for both early season herbicides and insecticide spraying later on you're asking for trouble.

Temperature, weather-wise, is another important factor to keep in mind especially when applying the liquid herbicides. On a hot day, many of the liquid formulations can volatize (evaporate into a gaseous state). They can then be absorbed through leaf pores by just about any plant that's nearby. The result of such invisible drifting can be fatal to your flowers and vegetables and it can be pretty deforming to trees, shrubs and vines. (Typically herbicide damage on preferred plants causes thickened, rolled, curling leaves, twisted tips on the newest growth and occassionally deformity so severe, the leaves take on a totally different shape than normal leaves.)

Finally in this discussion on herbicides let's consider the duration of effectiveness and the residue that's left behind when an herbicide is used. As mentioned earlier the pre-emergence herbicides intentionally leave a barrier behind - else they wouldn't work. Yet their chemical presence does no harm to your preferred plants; in short, they are compatible. There are herbicides that leave a full season's worth of residue behind that's damaging to any and all plants that try to grow (or re-grow) after application. Such herbicides are used to treat gravel driveways, dirt roads, etc. Their residue can (and often does) move horizontally through the soil due to grade changes and the resulting drainage after a rain fall. Improper use of such an herbicide can put it where you don't want it— and that's bad! Even our most common lawn weed killers which are selective herbicides, carry label warnings not to reseed after use for approximately 6-8 weeks.

WITHOUT HERBICIDES

If you wish to control weeds without herbicides, you can be successful. A thick layer of an organic mulch will help prevent weed growth and increase soil quality. Repeated light cultivation (hoeing) of soil after your garden is planted will slice off weeds, eliminating them while they're young. And a well fed lawn that's thick and lush will actually crowd out most weeds. Keeping your lawn a bit tall will also help to shade out crab grass. Remember, man has cultivated the land for hundreds of years and had herbicides at his disposal only a fraction of that time.

THE MOST POPULAR WEEDS

In closing, let's look at the "Top 13" weeds of our area:

POKEWEED

POKEWEED

Suddenly up in your garden, grows a 6 ft. tall weed with a red, hollow stem, and clusters of white flowers that eventually go on to be purple-black berries. It's pokeweed. A perennial that's sometimes difficult to eliminate — it's one of our showiest weeds! Parts of the plants are poisonous — so get rid of it by non-selective herbicides.

BARNYARD GRASS   GOOSE FOOT

BARNYARD GRASS

Like quack grass, barnyard grass is a clumpy, coarse fast growing monocot. Areas that flood seasonally, are prone to barnyard grass. And certainly it does grow in barnyards. Spot treatment with a non-selective herbicide will eliminate barnyard grass. Some gardeners try to remove it by digging — but that's a long, difficult process.

GOOSEFOOT

This weed is a dense grower, due to its ability to produce tens of thousands of seeds per plant. An introduced weed, goosefoot, was and still is grown as a pot herb. Varying from 1 to 6 feet in height this group forms dense thickets in fields, gardens and along road-sides and driveways. Control is best achieved by hoeing (removal) before the plants flower and go to seed.

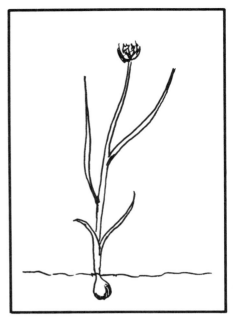

THISTLE   WILD ONION

THISTLES

Everyone knows thistles by the spines on their leaves and flower heads. Thistles vary in height from 2 to 6 feet. The worst of this group is the Canadian Thistle. Spot treatment with a non-selective herbicide is the way to eliminate thistles from lawns, gardens and roadsides.

WILD ONION

Wild onion and its relatives number some 300 species of aromatic (stinky) spring growers that seem to pop-up everywhere. Perennials that grow each year from a tiny bulb, wild onions are a nuisance especially in lawns. Some gardeners say their presence indicates the soil's need for lime. Broad leafed weed killers will give you the edge, but several applications will be necessary.

KNOTWEED

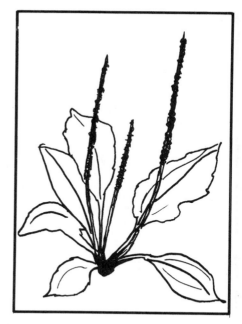

PLANTAGO RUGELLI

KNOTWEED

Tightly compacted soils of path or walk ways are the home of knotweed. This tough little weed forms a dense mat due to its prostrate growth habit. Tough, wiry stems with small leaves, knotweed is troublesome in both gardens and lawns.

PLANTAINS

Every lawn will at one time or another have a plantain problem. The plantains include perennials, biennial and annual forms. A low rosette of foliage with one or two tough, slender flower stalks, plantains are survivors of even the sharpest lawn mowers. Broadleaf weed killers are the key.

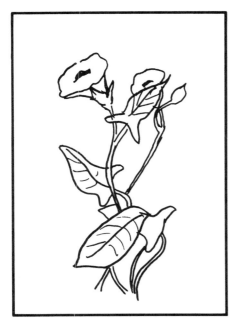

BINDWEED

DANDELION

BINDWEED

Also known as field morning-glory, bindweed can take up to 3-4 years to eliminate. The twirling stems wrap themselves around any plant that will stand in their way. Characterized by the typical trumpet shaped flowers and arrowhead leaves this persistent weed relies on a far reaching excessively deep root system for its almost indestructible quality. Spot treatment using a non-selective herbicide.

DANDELION

One of our most common and always recognized weeds, dandelions seem to grow everywhere. Most hated in lawns, dandelions are difficult to control due to their deep taproot and their prolific seed producing capability. A broadleaf weed killer for lawns will generally do them in.

CRABGRASS

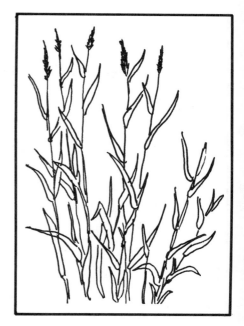

QUACKGRASS

CRABGRASS

Crabgrass is the favorite weed of suburban homeowners who just love their lawns! Annuals by nature, they're gone after a frost in the fall but they leave behind a legacy of literally thousands of seeds borne on each crabgrass plant. A tough, low, spoke-style growth habit makes them easily recognized. Mow your lawn a bit high and shade them out! Pre-emergence herbicides are very effective when applied in the spring before seeds germinate.

QUACKGRASS

Like most of the grassy weeds, quackgrass can be chopped, hoed, cut to tiny pieces, even lifted from the soil - only to go on living by regrowth of the segments re-rooting. It's horrible in lawns and gardens! Use of a non-selective weed killer, spot-applications though, directly on the clumps of quackgrass will, after repeated applications, eliminate it.

GROUND IVY

POISON IVY

GROUND IVY

Once ground ivy appears <u>anywhere</u> it's a problem. The stems of this obnoxious vine are nearly square. Leaves have a scalloped edge and the flowers are a medium lavender color.

'Everytime ground ivy is cut it'll re-root and spread even more.

<u>Repeated</u> applications of broadleaf weed killers are just about your only recourse - and even then your success is tenuous.

POISON IVY

Anyone who's gotten an ichy rash due to their exposure to poison ivy will tell you all about this "the worst of all" weeds. To avoid this weed keep in mind the phrase "leaflets three; let it be," as poison ivy's glossy attractive growth can appear along roadways, in stone walls, and climb up your shade trees.

Chemical control measures are necessary.

12

Pest Identification

By Mark Adams

As we go to press, the pesticide industry is in a state of flux. Chemicals are being re-evaluated, and some of the compounds available now may soon be restricted or banned. There is no need to dwell on methods of pest control in this publication. If you can positively identify a particular pest that is damaging your crop, the battle is more than half over. Consult your Dutchess County Cooperative Extension office for the proper control procedures, or visit a local garden center to see if your crop, and the identified pest, are listed on the label of a general use pesticide. If they are both listed, follow label directions precisely to control the pest. Remember: Always read the label.

Here are the pests you're most likely to meet if you garden in Dutchess County:

APHIDS

Small, brown, green black or red, soft body, winged or wingless

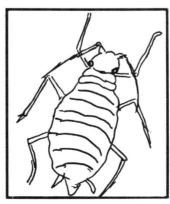

Widespread, on stems or under-sides of leaves; tomato, spinach, eggplant, peppers, carnation, rose, many others

JAPANESE BEETLE

½ inch, shiny green and brown adult

Rose, many other flowers, corn silk. Grubs feed on roots of lawn grasses

EUROPEAN CORN BORER

Inch-long white or tan caterpillar

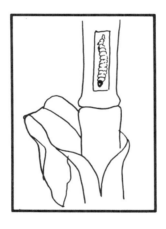

Bores inside stems of corn, pepper, zinnia, dahlia, chrysanthemum, fruit of corn and pepper

CORN EAR WORM

1-2 inches long, green or brown with lengthwise stripes

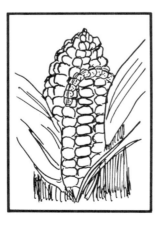

Silk and ear tips of corn, fruit of tomato

SQUASH VINE BORER

Wrinkled white cat-
erpillar with brown
head

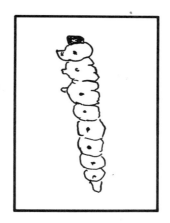

Bores inside vines
of squash, melon,
cucumber

FLEA BEETLE

Tiny black beetle,
jumps when
disturbed

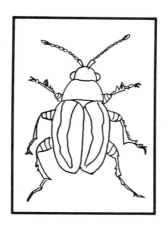

Chews small holes
in leaves of egg-
plant, tomato,
radish, turnips,
mustard and others

EASTERN TENT CATERPILLAR

Large hairy cater-
pillar, lives in a web
in the forks of trees
in early spring

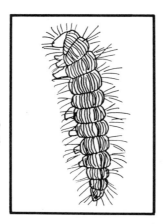

Defoliates trees,
especially apple,
crabapple and
cherry

GYPSY MOTH

Large hairy caterpillar, with blue, then red raised dots on body surface

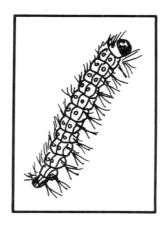

Defoliates most species of trees, feeding heavily in mid-summer

IMPORTED CABBAGE WORM

Up to one-inch long green worm, hides along stems and leaf veins

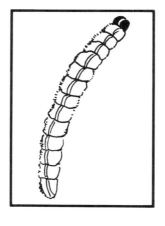

Chews holes in cabbage leaves, also broccoli, cauliflower, brussel sprouts, kale, collards, sweet alyssum

CUTWORM

Brown, hairless caterpillar, curled up just beneath soil surface

Widespread, cuts plants off at soil surface

SPRUCE BUDWORM

Dark brown cater-
pillars, spin webs
over needles of
evergreen trees

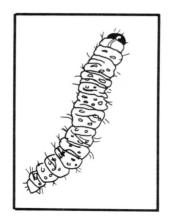

Feed on young
buds of most ever-
green trees and
shrubs

CABBAGE ROOT MAGGOT

Tiny white maggot

Chews roots of cab-
bage and its rela-
tives, including
broccoli and rad-
ishes, causing
plants to wilt

LEAF MINER

Tiny white grub.
Chews distinctive
channels between
upper and lower
leaf surfaces.

Spinach, beet,
chard

TWO-SPOTTED SPIDER MITE

Looks like dust to the naked eye, spins webs in severe infestations

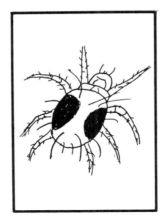

Under leaves of eggplant, rose, impatiens, salvia, marigold, ageratum. Prefers hot dry conditions.

GARDEN SLUG

Slimy snail without a shell

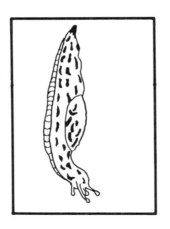

Feeds at night on leaves of marigold, salvia, pepper and other garden plants

WHITEFLY

Tiny white moth, seen in large groups on undersides of leaves

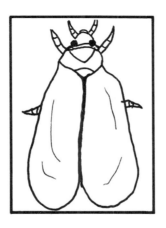

Tomato, squash, peppers, impatiens

OTHER PESTS

Other insect pests you might encounter include Colorado potato beetle on eggplant, potato or tomato, cucumber beetle (striped or spotted) on cucumber, fall armyworm on corn or shrubs, and leafhoppers on various garden plants.

FURRY PESTS

Dutchess County is home to a small menagerie of furry garden pests that can be more troublesome than the insects (since they have much bigger mouths).

• Deer — are putting some farmers right out of business. Their numbers have been increasing so fast in recent years that doe permits are being issued to hunters. Deer will eat anything in the garden, frequently wiping out a crop in one meal. They girdle young trees, especially during the winter, when the tender bark is a treat. Now that deer are suspected of playing host to ticks carrying Lyme disease, let's hope that steps are taken to decrease their numbers. Some farmers swear that stockings filled with human hair will repel deer.

• Woodchucks — these furry mammals burrow and establish a home near the garden, and feed first on tender plants nearest their hole, usually in the evening. They rarely eat tomato plants, so these can be planted near the garden edge.

• Raccoons — a threat to mature fruit and vegetables, especially sweet corn.

• Mice — they will chew holes in mature fruit and vegetables, even tomatoes. They burrow under the snow, girdling young trees (a wire screen will stop them) and chewing tulip and other bulbs (mice won't eat daffodils). Heavy garden mulching can encourage mice.

• Moles and skunks — often get the blame for digging up lawns. They are actually feeding on grubs in the lawn, so a properly maintained lawn will not attract these animals.

• Birds — feathered, not furry, but still a bad pest. Crows and red winged blackbirds are adept at digging up seeds, and many species of birds will eat cherries, strawberries and other fruits. Of course, birds also consume numerous insect pests.

DISEASES

Some of the most common plant diseases found in Dutchess County:

• Pythium: a fungus disease which is commonly known as "damp-off" when it mows down young seedlings. Attacks the roots and moves up the stem, causing a soft brown rot.

• Rhizoctonia: a white fungus which grows on the soil surface, attacking stems at the soil line. A problem on seedlings and mature impatiens plants.

• Anthracnose: black spots on tomato and other fruit, and lower branch dieback on dogwoods are caused by this fungus.

• Blight: early and late blight are a problem on tomato, potato and other vegetable plants. Lower leaves turn yellow or brown.

• Wilt: verticillium and fusarium wilt are problem diseases on tomato and eggplant; the letters (VF) after a variety name indicate resistance to these wilts.

• Mosaic: a stubborn virus that lingers in the soil, infects plants and is spread by sucking insects. Plants are stunted, with mottled and curled leaves. Some striped tulips are bred with a variety-specific virus that gives the flower its unusual appearance.

• Botrytis: grey mold; it attacks flowers, especially of petunia and geranium, and leaves, in damp weather.

• Black spot: fairly common on the leaves of roses in cool spring or fall weather.

• Mildew: a white mold observed on rose stems and leaves, and on leaves of squash or pumpkins, especially in cool damp weather.

• See chapter 10 for diseases of turf, and chapter 8 for diseases of tree fruits.

13

Gardens to Visit

By Terra Albertson

Hudson Valley gardening enthusiasts need not travel far to enjoy a wide variety of horticultural displays. From Mohonk Mountain House in New Paltz to the New York Botanical Garden in the Bronx, gardens and exhibits abound. City, county and town parks are always bursting with color during the growing season. The following selections of educational and display gardens are located within Dutchess County:

INNISFREE GARDEN

Location: Tyrrel Road, Millbrook, New York

Hours: Wednesday, Thursday, Friday - 10:00 am until 4:00 pm
              Saturday, Sunday - 11:00 a.m. until 5:00 p.m.
              Legal Holidays — 11:00 a.m. until 5:00 p.m.

Admission: $1.50 for people 16 years and over on weekends. No charge on Wednesday, Thursday, Friday and legal holidays.

Description: Innisfree Garden was designed and built by Walter Beck. To create what is called in the East a "cup garden," Beck used streams and waterfalls, terraces and retaining walls and rocks so poised as to keep specific areas in tension or in motion—taking from nature what he needed to make a work of art.

LOCUST GROVE

Location: 370 South Road, Poughkeepsie, New York

Hours: Open Memorial Day Weekend through September. Wednesday through Sunday - 10:00 am until 4:00 pm

Admission:

Adults	$3.00
Children, 7-16	$1.00
Children under 7	Free

Description: Locust Grove at the Young-Morse Historic Site contains an herb garden, ribbon garden, a French formal garden and an experimental garden where varieties are tested before planting in show gardens.

MADAM BRETT HOMESTEAD MUSEUM

Location: 50 Van Nydeck Avenue, Beacon, New York

Hours: Open May through October Friday, Saturday, Sunday - 11:00 am until 4:00 pm

Admission:

Adults	$2.00
Children	$1.00

Description: The "Marion Brinckerhoff Foster Memorial Garden," named in memory of a descendant of Madam Brett, is a formal Dutch garden with plants of the period (1709 through the American Revolution). In spring, the garden contains all tulips. In summer annual and perennial flowers, and herbs are on display. A wildflower garden is located in the woods near the house. Landscaping around the house is also from this period.

The New York Botanical Garden
MARY FLAGLER CARY ARBORETUM

Location: Route 44A, Millbrook, New York

Hours: Monday thru Saturday - 9:00 am until 4:00 pm Sunday - 1:00 pm until 4:00 pm

Admission: No admission. A permit is required to visit the grounds; can be obtained form the Visitors Office.

Description: The Arboretum's natural and horticultural displays include The Meadow Garden, Wappingers Creek Trail which passes through a wide range of habitats—old fields, forests, marshes and streams and a Scotch Pine alle'e; Cary Pines Trail; The Fern Glen which displays 125 species and varieties of native, European and Asian ferns; The Howard Taylor Lilac Collection which blooms from about mid-May until early June; The Perennial Garden, a living demonstration of good use of low maintenance perennials; greenhouse and nursery and plant science building.

THE ELEANOR ROOSEVELT CENTER AT VAL-KILL

Location: Route 9G, Hyde Park, New York; access by shuttle only from Home of Franklin D. Roosevelt

Hours: Open April through October, 7 days a week
9:00 am until 5:00 pm

Admission: Adults $1.95
Children, ages 4-15 $1.10

Description: During your self-guided tour, observe the gardens maintained for cut flowers and enjoy the quiet wooded pond and fields.

THE FRANKLIN D. ROOSEVELT LIBRARY AND MUSEUM

Location: Route 9, Hyde Park, New York

Hours: 9:00 am until 5:00 pm every day, except Thanksgiving, Christmas and New Year's Day

Admission: Grounds free
$2.00 for combination ticket to the library, Roosevelt Home, and Vanderbilt Mansion

Description: The Rose Garden and Perennial and Annual Garden exhibit many of the same varieties of plants grown during Roosevelt's time and are maintained in the same style. Trees growing on this lovely estate are also labeled.

STONY KILL FARM

Location: Route 9D, Wappingers Falls, New York

Hours: Monday thru Friday - 8:30 am until 4:30 pm and for special weekend programs.

Admission: Free

Description: Stony Kill Farm with its 750 acres of rolling country-side, farmland and woodlands offers the visitor three trails—Verplanck Farm Trail where both past and presentday farming techniques and crop types can be observed; Twin Trunks Trail, which exposes the hiker to a variety of habitats typical of the area, including deciduous forest, swamp and field; and Sierra Trails, a mixed habitat zone. Organic garden plots are available for community use for a fee. The center offers many educational services and special programs to the public.

THE VANDERBILT MANSION HISTORIC SITE

Location: Route 9, Hyde Park, New York

Hours: Open daily - 10:00 am until 6:00 pm

Admission: Grounds—Free
$2.00 for combination ticket to the Library, Roosevelt Home and Vanderbilt Mansion

Description: The estate garden represents an elegant expression of the lifestyle observed by the wealthy Hudson River Valley landowners in the late 1800's and early 1900's. The Italian Gardens are characterized by ornamental fountains, terraces, statues and loggia and a formal blending of flowers, trees, shrubs and vines. The Frederick W. Vanderbilt Garden Association has been able to cull from the estate garden records to duplicate many of the original plantings.

THE VASSAR ARBORETUM

Location: Raymond Avenue, Poughkeepsie, New York
(Vassar College)

Hours: Open year-round

Admission: Free

Description: It has been an ancient and honored tradition at Vassar for the sophomore class to plant or choose a tree and designate it with a marker. This tradition has created one of the most extensive collections of tree varieties on the East Cost. Also available are a Shakespear Garden, Perennial Garden, Daffodil Garden (test garden) and a greenhouse with a display of exotic plants.

FRESH HERB FARM

Location: Greig Farm, Pitcher Lane, Red Hook, New York
              (914) 758-5595

Hours: Open May thru October
              Thursday thru Sunday - 9:30 am until 5:00 pm

Admission: Free

Description: The Herb Walk consists of 18 demonstration gardens
              with more than 200 varieties of herbs and perennial
              flowers. The theme gardens provide a seasonal
              display of color.

DUTCHESS COUNTY COOPERATIVE EXTENSION

Location: Farm & Home Center, Route 44, Millbrook, New York
              Telephone: Agriculture — 677-5006
                         Horticulture — 677-5067

Hours: Master Gardeners are available to answer gardening
              questions, 9:00 am until 12:00 noon, Monday thru
              Friday. The resources of Cornell University are
              available to the Cooerative Extension agents to assist
              in testing soil and identifying pest and disease pro-
              blems. Literature and publications covering a wide
              variety of gardening topics are available through the
              Extension Office.

GARDEN CLUBS

Among the many garden clubs in Dutchess County are the following members of the Federated Garden Clubs of New York State:

              Dutchess Garden Study Club (Poughkeepsie)
              Nine Partners Garden Club (Millbrook)
              Old Dutchess Village Garden Club (Red Hook)
              Rhinebeck Garden Club (Rhinebeck)
              Stanford Garden Club (Stanfordville)
              Tioranda Garden Club (Fishkill-Beacon)
              Pine Plains Garden Club (Pine Plains)

DUTCHESS COUNTY FAIR

The Dutchess County Fair is held annually during late August, at the fairgrounds in Rhinebeck. Gardeners and farmers can enter their locally grown flowers, fruits and vegetables in the following categories:

Horticulture

Flowers (cut or potted), including marigold, zinnia, geranium, flowering house plant, wildflower bouquet, perennial, tuberous begonia.

Roses
Gladiolus
Floral Design.

Vegetables

Beets
Lima Beans
String Beans
Broccoli
Cabbage
Carrots
Cauliflowr
Chard, Swiss
Cucumber
Eggplant
Leek
Lettuce
Muskmelon
Onion

Parsley
Peppers
Pumpkin
Radishes
Rhubarb
Rutabaga
Ornamental vegetables
Squash
Sweet Corn
Tomatoes
Turnips
Watermelon
Any other vegetable
Melon, any other type
Potatoes

Fruits

Apples
Pears
Plums

Peaches
Grapes
Berries

14

About the Authors

Mark Adams is the owner/operator of a 50,000 square foot greenhouse business in Poughkeepsie, where he and his staff produce more than one million annual, perennial and vegetable plants each year. Mark was raised on his father's fruit farm in Salt Point, and has managed the vegetable production of Adams Fairacre Farm, winning several grand-champion vegetable ribbons at the Dutchess County Fair. He is also a garden writer for area newspapers.

Terra Albertson is a life long resident of the Hudson Valley who tends her annual and perennial gardens at her home in LaGrange. She is currently employed at a local greenhouse/nursery operation.

Steve Clarke is a 6th generation fruitgrower in Milton. He graduated from Michigan State University in 1966 with a B.S. Cum Laude in Horticulture. Steve lives on the Clarke Homestead with his wife Judy and their three children Pam, Brad and Kelly. Their Pick Your Own operation, called Prospect Hill Orchards, has 150 acres of cherries, peaches, pears and apples in production. Steve has been active in industry and fruit research groups.

Sandy Greig owns the Fresh Herb Farm in Red Hook, N.Y. As a designer, she's worked in the varying mediums of textiles, architecture and horticulture. Sandy has written three books on herbs and everlasting flowers and writes a craft column for the Living with Herbs newsletter, an international publication. Her gardens have been featured in McCall's and Self magazines, The Herb Book and Reader's Digest's Herbal Magic. Sandy is a part-time student at Bard College and studies creative writing and transpersonal psychology, the integration of eastern and western thought.

Joann Gruttadaurio has degrees in Agronomy from S.U.N.Y. at Cobleskill and Cornell University, as well as a Masters of Professional Studies in Education from Cornell University. She has worked for the last 13 years for Cornell Cooperative Extension as an Extension Associate with responsibilities in educational resource development for Commercial greenhouse, nursery and turfgrass professionals.

Joe Indelicato — "Everything's going modern, but I still like the horse-and-carriage days," says Joe, who still lives on the farm in Highland where he was born, and who still raises grapes, strawberries, raspberries, figs and vegetables, all cultivated with his horse-drawn equipment.

Ruth Link is a long-time resident of Dutchess County. She is chairperson of Cooperative Extension Agriculture Program Committee, and is a Master Gardener. Ruth spends her spare time in her extensive annual flower and vegetable garden, and raises many varieties from seed.

Stephanie Mallozzi is the Commercial Horticulture and Consumer Turf Specialist with Cornell Cooperative Extension of Dutchess County, a position she has held for the past six years. Prior to that, she was a horticultural consultant with Rockland County Cooperative Extension. Stephanie received her Associates and International Baccalaureate Degrees from Rockland Community College and her B.S. degree from Cook College, Rutgers University. She and her husband Andy and son Chad reside in Hopewell Junction.

Carl Norton began his work in the field of landscape design in 1962 in Denmark, working as a draftsman for a landscape architect. There he received extensive schooling in working with road designs and contour plants. After returning to the states in 1965, he took a course in building architecture and then began working under the supervision of Powers Taylor at Rosedale Nurseries. He received further training as a draftsman, and also took extensive schooling there including courses from Penn State University in the Horticulture and Agricultural Department relating to the study of various plants, plant identification and uses. In all, he spent close to three years engaged in intensive study in the landscape and landscape design field before he began dealing with the public as a professional landscape designer. In 1969 he became the manager of the Landscape and Landscape Design Department of Rosedale Nurseries in Millbrook. In 1970 he continued his landscape design training by studying Oriental landscape design in Tokyo, Kyoto, Taipei, (Formosa) and Hong Kong. From the years 1971-1974 he continued to attend seminars through Cornell University School of Agriculture and Horticulture, including numerous courses in landscape design and related fields. Since 1975, Carl has volunteered with the Cooperative Extension of Cornell University in Millbrook and in 1975 was placed on the Advisory Committee for Horticulture. In 1985 he received a "Special Recognition" Award for leadership, cooperation and service from the Cooperative Extension of Dutchess County. In 1978 he received a certificate to teach adult education at B.O.C.E.S. in the field of landscape design and continues to teach courses there to this day. In 1976 Carl started "Landscape Concepts" in the Millbrook area where he has continued to practice his profession since that time.

Bob Piggott, owner of Piggott's Farm Market, is the winner of 15 grand-champion ribbons in the vegetable division of the Dutchess County Fair. Bob graduated from Wappingers Central School and Oswego State Technical College, and received his M.A. degree from T.C.-Columbia University. He taught Industrial Arts for 31 years, until his retirement from teaching in 1986. Bob resides in Poughkeepsie with his wife Trudy. They have two sons, Mark and Jim.

145

Sandra Reilly is an active Master Gardener at Dutchess County Cooperative Extension. She attended horticultural education courss at Bronx Botanical Gardens, including Landscaping with Perennials, Care of Perennials and Basic Botony. Sandra has taught gardening courses at Marist College, Arlington Adult Education and Cary Arboretum. Sandra was manager of the greenhouse at Adams Fairacre Farms for 2½ years and of the Carey Arboretum Plant Shop for 2 years, and tends her own large perennial garden at her home in LaGrange.

Gary Zinsmeyer is the Dutchess County Cooperative Extension Agent working in the area of consumer horticulture. He hosts a T.V. series airing from NYC to Albany on the Cablevision Network and also prepares seasonal gardening articles and radio shows of a call-in format. A Cornell graduate, Gary has served in the New York State Cooperative Extension system since 1975. Prior to Extension work, Gary developed a vocational horticulture program for high school students and adults in Syracuse, N.Y. His floral design expertise is the result of his training at Alfred State College and his years serving as a Floral Shop Manager in upstate New York.

Index